THE FAMILY CREATIVE WORKSHOP

18

Square Dancing, Stagecraft
Stained Glass, Stamp Decoupage
Stenciling
Stone Painting, Street Games
String Art, Structural Furnishings
Sugar Shapes

Plenary Publications International, Inc.
New York and Amsterdam

Published by Plenary Publications International, Incorporated 300 East 40th Street, New York New York 100 16, for the Blue Mountain Crafts Council.

Library of Congress Catalog Card Number: 73-89331. Complete set International Standard Book Number: 0-88459-021-6. Volume 18 International Standard Book Number: 0-88459-017-8.

Manufactured in the United States of America. Printed and bound by the W. A. Krueger Company, Brookfield, Wisconsin.

Printing preparation by Lanman Lithoplate Company.

Publishers:
Plenary Publications International, Incorporated
300 East 40th Street
New York, New York 10016

Steven Schepp
EDITOR-IN-CHIEF

Jerry Curcio
PRODUCTION MANAGER

Peggy Anne Streep
VOLUME EDITOR

Joanne Delaney
EDITORIAL ASSISTANT

Editorial preparation:
Tree Communications, Inc.
250 Park Avenue South
New York, New York 10003

Rodney Friedman
EDITORIAL DIRECTOR

Ronald Gross
DESIGN DIRECTOR

Paul Levin
DIRECTOR OF PHOTOGRAPHY

Jill Munves
TEXT EDITOR

Sonja Douglas
ART DIRECTOR

Rochelle Lapidus
Marsha Gold
DESIGNERS

Lucille O'Brien
EDITORIAL PRODUCTION

Ruth Forst Michel
COPYREADER

Eva Gold
ADMINISTRATIVE MANAGER

Editors for this volume:
Andrea DiNoto
STAGECRAFT

Donal Dinwiddie
STRUCTURAL FURNISHINGS

Linda Hetzer
SQUARE DANCING
STRING ART

Nancy Bruning Levine
STAINED GLASS
STENCILING

Marilyn Nierenberg
STAMP DECOUPAGE
STONE PAINTING
STREET GAMES

Mary Grace Skurka
SUGAR SHAPES

Originating editor of the series:
Allen Davenport Bragdon

Contributing photographers:
Erik Erikson
Jay Keene
Steven Mays

Contributing editor:
Barbara Daye

Contributing illustrators:
Thom Augusta
Marina Givotovsky
Patricia Lee
Lynn Matus
Sally Shimizu

Production:
Thom Augusta
Christopher Jones
Patricia Lee

Sylvia Sherwin
Leslie Strong
Gregory Wong

Photo and illustration credits:
STAGECRAFT: All photographs, except those on pages 2194, 2195, and black and white photographs, pages 2214 and 2215, are by Jay Keene; photograph by Jay Keene, page 2207, courtesy of KaiDib Films International, Glendale, California. STAINED GLASS: Photograph, page 2216, courtesy of the French Government Tourist Office, New York, New York; photographs, page 2219, courtesy of Blenko Glass Company, Inc., Milton, West Virginia; stained glass samples, page 2218, courtesy S. A. Bendheim Company, Inc., New York, New York. STAMP DECOUPAGE: Photograph, page 2232, of the penny magenta, courtesy of Irwin Weinberg, Wilkes Barre, Pennsylvania. STENCILING: Stenciled floor, page 2250, courtesy of Daisy Two Gift Shop, Florham Park, New Jersey; stenciled floor, page 2251, courtesy of The Museum of Early Trades and Crafts, Madison, New Jersey. SUGAR SHAPES: Sugar wonderland, pages 2300 and 2301, designed and made by Marina Givotovsky and Lynn Matus.

Acknowledgement:
STREET GAMES: The editors wish to express their appreciation to the members of the Boy's Club of New York, East 111th Street, New York, for their cooperation in the preparation of this entry.

The Project-Evaluation Symbols appearing in the title heading at the beginning of each project have these meanings:

Range of approximate cost:
¢ Low: under $5 or free and found natural materials

$ Medium: about $10

$$ High: above $15

Estimated time to completion for an unskilled adult:
⊠ Hours

🕐 Days

1/30 Weeks

Suggested level of experience:
🧍 Child alone

👪 Supervised child or family project

🧍 Unskilled adult

🧍 Specialized prior training

Tools and equipment:
🔨 Small hand tools

🔧 Large hand and household tools

🔬 Specialized or powered equipment

On the cover:
This portion of a leaded stained glass panel incorporates glass of several types and colors. See the entry "Stained Glass," beginning on page 2216. Stained-glass panel by Erik Erikson. Photograph by Paul Levin.

**Contents and
craftspeople for Volume 18:**

SQUARE DANCING
Swing Your Partner

Lee Kopman's first contact with square dancing came when he was in college; it was a required course for his degree in physical education and recreation from Adelphi University, New York. His interest led him to take private instructions; he then started teaching children to dance. Lee has been a square-dance caller for more than 20 years, traveling around the United States and Canada, and has made a number of caller recordings on the Blue Star label. His tapes and a glossary of square-dance calls that he compiled are widely distributed. Lee has originated nearly 100 square dance figures, and he continues to choreograph new steps.

Additional helps

If you want to master all 75 basic square-dance figures, you can do so in one of the 5,000 square-dance clubs in the United States. For the name of the nearest club, write Roy and Marita Davis, 3320 Cornelia Drive, Louisville, Kentucky 40220.

To keep up with square dancers around the country, you can do so with two magazines: **Square Dancing**, official publication of The Sets in Order, American Square Dance Society, 462 North Robertson Blvd., Los Angeles, Ca. 90048; and **American Square Dance**, Box 788, Sandusky, Ohio 44870.

If you would like to start a reference library, you can order a **Glossary of Square-Dance Calls** by Lee Kopman, 2965 Campbell Ave., Wantagh, N. Y. 11793. To find out which square-dance figures are on a given square-dance record, you can order **The Encyclopedia of Singing Call Records** by Jim and Jean Cholmondeley, 301 SW 74th St., Lawton, Oklahoma 73501.

"Square your sets. First couple bow and swing. Allemande left your corner, then swing your partner and promenade home." Thus a night of square dancing begins. This type of dancing is sometimes considered a uniquely American form of folk dance, but it has a long history in other parts of the world.

Dancing in a square was a part of French court ballet in the early eighteenth century. Called a quadrille, it was a precision dance performed by couples in a square formation. The various dance steps were fixed and memorized by the dancers, who were taught by dance masters to execute smooth, flowing movements. Quadrilles spread across the channel and became well established in the British Isles, then found their way to America. There the same basic dance steps were used, but the dances were modified to allow more couples to participate.

Late in the eighteenth century, square dancing became a popular social activity in many rural areas of the United States. In church halls, barns, and firehouses, the weekly square dance, usually on Saturday night, brought family, friends, and neighbors together for fun and fellowship. Without formal instruction, most of the couples danced their own unique versions of the quadrilles. In dispensing with French terms, they called them square dances. A man with a strong and pleasing voice would act as caller, leading the dancers to the tune of a lone fiddle or accordion player. To cover any deficiencies in the music and to lighten the drill-type dancing, the caller kept up a continuous teasing patter while the dance went on. As the dances were Americanized, so were the names of the steps. *Allemande* is a French dance term adapted from a German hand-holding dance, but the callers gave the word an American pronunciation. They did the same with *chasse*, the French word for chase or pursuit, which became sashay, and *dos-à-dos*, the French term for back-to-back, which became do-si-do. Simplifying the dancing while retaining the fundamental steps let callers and couples participate in square dances in different parts of the country.

At the beginning of the nineteenth century, many changes took place. Dress styles became more elaborate; so did dance styles. Square dancing moved into the ballroom, where it remained for a century. Early in the twentieth century, couple dances such as the polka and waltz replaced square dancing; the latter became a thing of the past. Then, in 1926, Mr. and Mrs. Henry Ford wrote *Good Morning—After a Sleep of Twenty-five Years, Old-Fashioned Dancing is Being Revived*. Lloyd Shaw, a Colorado school superintendent, read the Fords' book, and began to study square dancing. In 1939, he published *Cowboy Dances*, which filled in the gaps in the Ford book. He taught others how to teach square dancing, and the current wave of interest was on its way.

Eastern and Western Versions

Two square-dancing techniques have evolved in the U.S.; they are known as the Eastern and Western styles, although both are danced in all parts of the country. Eastern square dancing is the older of the two; one couple moves to the next couple and the four dancers execute a figure while other dancers maintain their positions until they, in turn, execute the same movement. This is sometimes called barn dancing. It calls for lots of swinging, foot stomping, and hand clapping; the noisy accompaniment sometimes drowns out the musicians. Western dancing is more complicated. It involves independent dancing, with two couples doing different things at the same time. For this, the dancers must listen closely to the caller; considerable skill and perfect timing are required, more than for the older dance. For Western-style dances, records usually provide the music. This gives the caller a more convenient means of supplying music and lets him choose any tempo he feels would work best with his choreography.

In a joyous square dance, men join right hands in the center to form a right-hand star (page 2186), while women on the outside of the square clap hands to the beat of the music.

The caller at the left, Lee Kopman, uses a public-address system to amplify his voice so all the dancers can hear his calls. Phonograph records provide the music.

The Caller

As with any organized activity, a square dance must have a leader. The caller performs this function. He is unique to American folk dance. When the square dance came to the United States, the fiddler called out cues to remind the dancers of the next step. The fiddler became a caller; in time the caller started to sing to the music, filling in with extra words between calls. This extemporaneous aspect of the dance is also unique to the United States.

The modern caller can be any man or woman who is a square-dance enthusiast, and who has a good voice, a sense of humor, and the patience to teach people fundamental as well as advanced steps. Although he must speak distinctly, he usually has the advantage of a public-address system to amplify his voice. The caller needs a sense of rhythm, timing, and continuity. He announces each action of the dance in sequence, giving the cue to the dancers just far enough ahead of time so the action can be executed to that part of the music chosen for it. In Western square dancing, the caller not only prompts the dancers to familiar figures; he becomes a choreographer by spontaneously improvising and calling steps in a new sequence. The caller knows what position the couples will be in after any given call, so he can control the dance by arranging his calls in any way that pleases him.

Lessons

No square dancer can dance to a caller's cues without training and practice. The dancers learn a special jargon that helps identify the various parts of the dance. A formation is the position assumed at the start of a figure. A figure is a basic sequence of square-dance movements that are executed in response to a call. A call is a cue or command given by the caller to let the dancers know what figures they should dance next. Dancers must listen to the caller's cues, and the caller is obliged to speak distinctly and to choose calls in a sequence that lets the dancers execute a smoothly choreographed dance. Novice dancers take at least 20 (and often 30) lessons. These once-a-week lessons have a formal class structure, with the caller

teaching the movements step-by-step. While attending the classes, the dancer is expected additionally to dance at least once a week. To do well on the dance floor, he eventually must master 75 basic square-dance figures. Levels of square dancing above this are reached by learning approximately 25 additional figures for each plateau until 200 figures are mastered. At this level is challenge dancing (page 2191); square dancers who reach this level sometimes dance five or six times a week.

Along with this time investment is a costume investment. Women usually make their own brightly colored, full-skirted dresses, and buy matching crinoline petticoats and ruffled pettipants. This is a square-dancing rule of etiquette; underwear that shows during dancing should match. Women wear flat-heeled shoes (high-heeled shoes would be too dangerous for vigorous square dancing). A man often matches his wife's colors, but he always wears a long-sleeved shirt so the women will not have to touch sweaty arms. Some men carry a tiny hand towel—in matching colors—tied to the belt.

The dancers respond to the caller's calls by dancing not only with their own partners but with the others who started in the original square of eight people.

The basic formations

Formations are like still photographs of the dancers' positions at the start of a dance figure. (Eleven such formations are pictured or diagrammed on pages 2186 and 2187). These are formations named so the position of each dancer relative to the others in the formation can be quickly identified. A formation can recur throughout a dance, and it can be repeated in combination with other formations. Occasionally a formation has a movement attached to it, so the dancers return to their original positions (as in "eight-chain-thru," page 2187). Sometimes the movement attached to a figure causes dancers to finish in an entirely new formation (as in "double-pass-thru," page 2187). Sometimes the formation is simply a starting position for any number of figures. The more common formations are shown on the next two pages.

Some basic formations

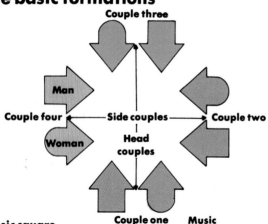

The basic square

The basic square formation is formed by four couples facing toward the center of their square. Couple number one have their backs to the music and the caller; couples two, three, and four are designated by going counterclockwise (to their right) around the square. The head couples are couples one and three. The side couples are two and four. At the call, "Square your set," the couples line up as shown in what are called the home positions.

Right-hand star

To dance a right-hand star, two or more dancers designated by the caller (in the photograph, the head couples) step from their home positions toward the center of the set. They extend right hands at shoulder level, join them, and walk in the direction they are facing (clockwise). Their joined hands serve as a pivot point.

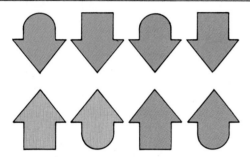

Lines of four

Through a series of calls, the dancers have reached a formation with two facing lines that have four dancers in each line. In each line, couples (indicated by matching colors) join hands with each other and with the adjacent couple.

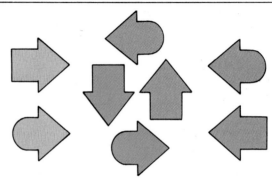

Left-hand star

Similar to the right-hand star shown above is the left-hand star, in which two or more dancers step toward the center and extend left hands at shoulder level, then walk in the direction they are facing (counterclockwise). Again, their joined hands serve as the pivot point.

Ocean wave

After a series of calls, the dancers have reached a new formation. In each line of four, the direction dancers face alternates. This is called an ocean wave. The couples are in two waves of four dancers each, with hands joined at shoulder level. Partners of a couple face the same direction with another dancer between them.

Alamo ring

An Alamo ring is an ocean wave that has been bent in at the ends to make a circle. Usually, dancers execute what is called an allemande left by giving a left hand to a member of the opposite sex; then they turn halfway around and join hands with the dancer on the right. In the Alamo ring, a man faces the opposite direction from his partner.

Allemande thar
In this formation, either all the men or all the women are in the center of the square, as determined by the sequence of calls. The men are usually there. Couples move around with a left forearm swing (joining forearms rather than hands) until the men can join right hands in a right-hand star formation in the center. To move in this position, the men back up in a counterclockwise direction while the women walk forward, also counterclockwise, each staying next to her partner.

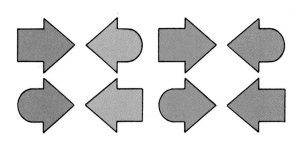

Eight-chain-thru
In this moving formation, the starting and ending positions are the same. Four couples are lined up, with two on the outside facing in and two on the inside back-to-back, facing out. Each dancer on the inside gives a right hand to the dancer faced, moves by, gives a left hand to a partner, and turns to face inward. Each dancer starting on the outside gives a right hand to the dancer faced, walks by, and gives a right hand to a dancer at the opposite end. This action is continued until all couples, moving simultaneously, finish at their starting points.

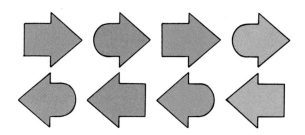

Single-file column
Through a series of calls, two lines are formed, one facing one way, the other facing the opposite direction. In each line, men and women alternate. Each dancer holds the hand of someone of the opposite sex, facing the opposite direction.

Diamond
Two couples join hands to form a right-hand star formation; the other two couples do the same. In both stars, the women line up and all join hands in a row.

Double pass-thru position
In starting this moving formation, four couples assemble so the head couples are at their home positions, as in the basic square, while the side couples are in the center facing each other.

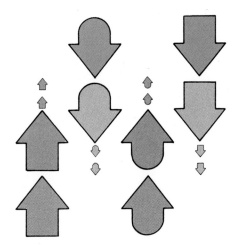

Double pass-thru movement
All couples move simultaneously. Each center couple passes through the first couple it faces, then moves on to pass through the second couple it faces. The outside couples follow the inside couples moving forward and passing.

Double pass-thru finish
When the movement diagrammed at left is completed, all couples are facing out, but the couples that were on the outside of the formation are now in the center.

2187

A singing call

An average night of square dancing lasts two and a half or three hours and is made up of eight segments called tips, each lasting ten or fifteen minutes, with a five-minute break between them. A tip includes both a singing call (illustrated on these pages) and a hash call (page 2191). A singing call is danced to any popular song that might be familiar. The song selected should have a melody that all the dancers know. The caller creates a special square-dance pattern to fit his singing call, planning and calling specific patterns for each song. His special pattern of square-dance figures is repeated four times, twice for the head couples and twice for the side couples. During calls set in advance that involve the entire square, such as "grand right and left" (giving right and left hands alternately around the square) or "promenade" (meeting your partner and walking back to your home position), the caller sings the song while the dancers perform the movements designated.

A singing call starts with an introductory set of movements involving all four couples in each square, while the caller sings the words of the song. Then he twice calls the pattern of figures created for the song for the head couples. The introductory movements are repeated, with the caller again singing the song. Then the pattern of figures is repeated twice more for the side couples. The dance ends with the repetition of introduction while the caller sings the song a third time.

Figures and illustrations that follow show the action in one such singing call.

Introduction

1: "Square your set."

2: "Bow to your partner."

3: "Bow to your corner." (Your "corner" is a person of the opposite sex who is part of the couple next to you.)

4: "Allemande left." (Give your left hand to your corner and make a half turn; then go back to your original position.)

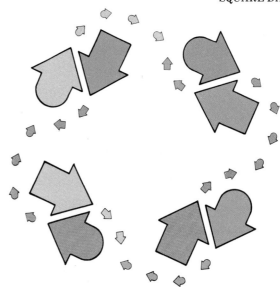

5: "Grand right and left." (Extend your right hand to your partner and walk by him or her. Then extend your left hand to the next person of the opposite sex (Figure A, right), and walk by.

A Figure A: Continue around the square, alternately extending your right and your left hand, until you meet your partner again.

6: "Swing your partner." (Holding each other as pictured, swing around each other, maintaining your position as a couple in relation to the other couples in the square.)

7: "Promenade back home." (Join right and left hands with your partner at waist level and walk around the square until you are back in your home position.)

Figure

8: "Heads lead to the right." (Head couples walk to the couple on their right.)

9: "Circle round." (Head couples join hands with the side couple they are facing, and all four walk in a circle.)

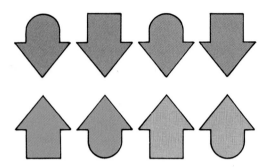

B
Figure B: "To a line of four." (The dancers break open the circle and form two lines of four, facing each other.)

10: "Star thru." (Men raise their right hands, women their left, and join them in an arch high above their heads.)

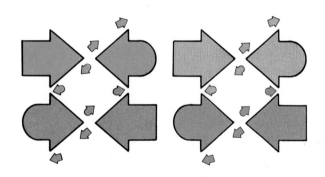

C
Figure C: Keeping hands joined, women walk through the arch and men walk around the women making a quarter turn in the completed "star thru."

11: "Right and left thru." (To begin this figure, couples join right hands and walk by each other.)

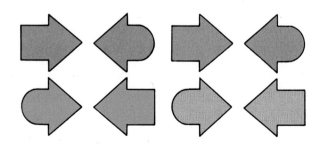

D
Figure D: Then each man faces his original partner, extends his left hand, places his right hand in the small of her back, and turns her counterclockwise to face the direction they both came from.

12: "Pass thru." (Each couple passes through the opposite couple, with each individual passing right shoulders with the person he or she is facing.)

13: After the pass-through is completed, the couples that were on the outside are on the inside and all have rejoined hands.

14: "Swing your corner." (Your "corner" is the person who was next to you at the corner of the original square.)

15: "Promenade your corner home." (Each man walks his corner to his home position; she then becomes his new partner.)

A hash call

The music for a hash call consists of chord progressions repeated over and over. The caller choreographs a dance on the spot, prompting the dancers as he improvises calls spontaneously. In a hash call, the caller cues the dancers on specific movements to be followed, filling in the call with a patter of words that usually rhyme and follow the music almost beat for beat. Ingenious callers often make up their own patter, the "hash," injecting humor and local references. Hash calling generally does not follow any repeating pattern of square-dance figures, although the caller may establish a specific sequence of steps in advance.

For the first level of square dancing, a dancer must be able to execute 75 figures that the caller can work into a hash call. As the dancers become more advanced, the caller increases the number of calls in what is known as challenge dancing. Most square-dance groups use about 125 basic figures in their weekly dances. Challenge dancers must know 200 to 400 figures. Dancers do not challenge each other; the dance itself is a challenge to all. There is no goal or objective to be reached other than to maintain the dancers' pleasure and interest. Challenge dancers are pleased if they are able to dance 80 percent of the time without having the square fall apart. To go through an entire evening without having a broken square means the figures are no longer a challenge. Challenge figures are not necessarily danced faster, but are made up of a greater variety of movements. A sequence of challenge dancing, pictured on page 2192, starts with "exploding the wave," followed by "men run" to get into position for "scoot back."

Exploding the wave

16: "Exploding the wave" starts with the four couples arranged in two waves.

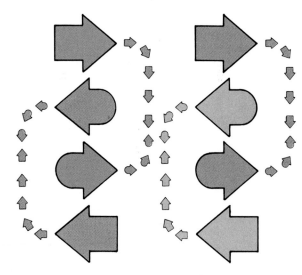

E
Figure E: Each dancer steps forward and makes a quarter turn inward.

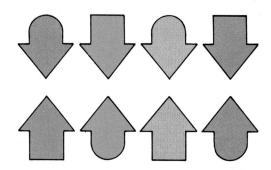

F
Figure F: The movement indicated in Figure E arranges the dancers in two lines that are perpendicular to the original wave lines. But in these lines, everyone is facing inward.

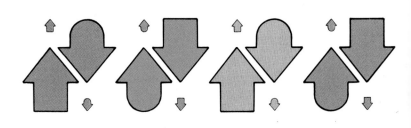

G
Figure G: Each dancer extends a right hand to the person opposite and performs what is called a right-hand pull-by.

17: After pulling by, the dancers are again in two lines of four, but everyone is facing out.

Men run

18: At the command, "Men run," the men step out and make a quarter turn to their right.

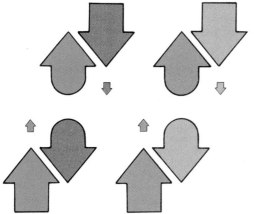

H

Figure H: The men make another quarter turn to their right and step between the women, joining right hands with them to complete the movement.

Scoot back

19: The command, "Scoot back," is given when two "ocean waves" have been formed, with the men facing in and the women facing out.

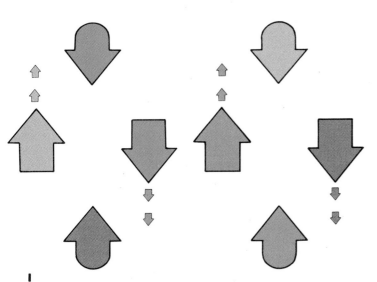

20: Each man steps forward to meet the man opposite, joining him with a forearm grip.

21: The men make half a turn to the right while the women, who were facing out, turn to face inward in the positions vacated by the men.

I

Figure I: Each man goes back to join hands with his original partner.

22: The result is two ocean-wave formations again, but this time the men are facing out and the women are facing in.

STAGECRAFT
Set Design and Stage Lighting

Theodore Abramov has a Master of Fine Arts degree from New York University and is an instructor of lighting design and technical production at Queens College, New York. His theater experience includes collegiate, amateur, and summer-stock shows, as well as Broadway and Off-Broadway productions. He has been a member of the A.P.A. Phoenix Repertory Company, toured with the Rolling Stones, and worked on the Woodstock Festival. He designed sets and lighting for Robert Anderson's play, Solitaire, *a showcase production at Lincoln Center in New York.*

Jay B. Keene, associate professor of design, Queens College, New York, received his Master of Fine Arts degree from the School of Drama, Yale University. He designed settings, costumes, and lighting for more than 200 theatrical productions for colleges, summer-stock shows, and Off-Broadway theaters. His sketches are part of permanent theatrical-design collections at Yale University and the Smithsonian Institution. His set designs appear on pages 2196, 2197, 2200, 2201, 2208, 2210, and 2215.

"The play's the thing," said Hamlet, though had the melancholy Dane been a scene or lighting designer, he might have added that the play's the thing for which one creates an environment. This setting, where actors perform and action unfolds, may be as real as a room with walls and furnishings, or as abstract as an empty stage with space defined only by light and shadow. As a design, it expresses the theme and mood of the play in accordance with the director's point of view. But as a construction, it must work for the actors who inhabit it. The artistry, skill, technical expertise, and knowledge of materials that go into the design and lighting of a stage set are embraced by the term stagecraft. This craft deals with the most concrete aspects of a theatrical production, but the final product is illusion.

Stagecraft may be examined in two categories—the design and construction of sets (pages 2196 through 2207), and stage lighting (pages 2208 through 2215). On a professional level, each is a vastly complex subject. But an aspiring designer need not feel intimidated; the best ideas are often the simplest. No matter what your budget or level of experience, it is useful to know how a professional approaches design problems; one method is described here. Craftnotes on the construction and painting of some specific scenic elements are on pages 2202 through 2207. In the lighting section (page 2208), a widely used approach to stage lighting is outlined. Technical knowledge in both areas is enormously helpful, but in the end good design is always based on imagination.

The type of theater ordinarily found in school and church auditoriums, with a raised stage and a curtain, is called a proscenium theater (see Types of Theaters, page 2204). Since this is the facility most widely used, all of the settings pictured here are designed for such a theater. But keep in mind that theater can be created anywhere—on a street corner or in a park, in a garage, gymnasium, or loft. Whatever the staging situation, the methods described here can be adapted to suit it.

While viewing the stage from the light booth, a lighting technician receives her cues through headphones as she sits at a manual control console, from which all stage lights are controlled. The cues are stored in the preset console at left and are called up electronically by the technician.

Opposite: A set designed by Theodore Abramov, representing a New York apartment and created for John Guare's *House of Blue Leaves*, is shown near completion at Queens College Theater in New York. In the foreground, the lighting designer sits at a work board in the center of the auditorium as he conducts a technical rehearsal. With an intercom, he cues the lighting technician in a booth above and behind the audience.

Jay Keene's rendering for *The Birds* by Aristophanes indicates style (abstract), set modules (platforms), color, and mood. The overall desired effect, that of an airy, fantastic mountaintop atmosphere, is well communicated. The completed set is shown opposite.

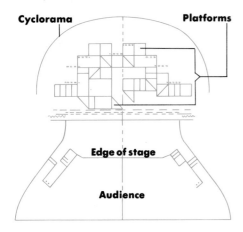

The ground plan for the actual set of *The Birds* shows the platforms drawn to scale on stage. Several ground plans for other types of sets are shown on pages that follow.

Performing Arts
Set design

Before an idea can be sketched or a hammer lifted, the set designer must observe one cardinal rule. He must read the play. This may seem obvious, but you would be surprised how often it is not done. The set designer cannot even rely on a director's synopsis; he must read the play himself with a pencil and pad at hand, noting the requirements from scene to scene. Playwrights sometimes give very specific indications of place and setting in stage directions. In this case, the set designer's job is simplified. Other playwrights give very little in the way of stage directions, leaving much to be gleaned from the dialogue. At this first reading, the only concern is establishing the concrete elements of time and place.

Time
The set designer notes the time of day or night. This may affect the shade and color of the scenery. In an indoor set, it will certainly affect what is visible through doors and windows. The time of year may be important; foliage will have a different appearance according to the season. If it is winter, a fireplace may have to seem to be in use. If the play is set in a particular period in history, this time element will be the most obvious factor dictating the style of architecture and decor.

Place
When the set designer has ascertained the general nature of the place, he then determines its specific nature. For example, if a scene takes place indoors, is it in someone's house? What room? Is it a store? What kind? Is it a business office, a warehouse, a bar? If the scene is to be played outdoors, is it in a forest, field, city street, country lane, or even outer space? Is the place real or imaginary? Is the house in a specific city? If so, the general style may be dictated. But if the location is specific and also well known, precise details of the actual place may have to be copied. If the location is undetermined, details may be left to the imagination.

The completed set for *The Birds* is faithful to the artist's original rendering, opposite. Pivoting wings were constructed so that actors could move them easily like partitions, thus changing and redefining the acting areas during the play.

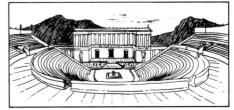

The ancient Greek dramas were presented in daylight in huge outdoor arenas, theaters in-the-round like the one shown above.

This type of pretty picture-frame setting was made famous by Inigo Jones in seventeenth-century England. His set and costume designs for Shakespearean productions are classics.

Theme

With notes in hand, the set designer discusses the play with the director. The director's concept of the play has a direct bearing on the set design. It is the director who determines and states the theme of the play to all actors and designers. This theme is the central idea expressed by the play as a whole. Often a playwright will suggest the theme in the play's title or dialogue, or he might just imply it by the action. In any case, it is the director's interpretation of the play's theme that must be expressed by the set. A spartan theme might be represented by a clean, uncluttered place with visual elements of a functional nature. A sensual theme, on the other hand, might require just the opposite: a plush, rich, overly decorative setting that suggests decadence. Once these elements of style have been determined, the set designer can begin to think about the nature of the space he must create.

Space and Style

Sophocles' *Oedipus Rex* is a Greek tragedy involving royal incest, patricide, and the upheaval of a great nation. These events seem to demand enormous space; so while the actual playing area will be limited, the job of the set designer is to create the illusion of great space. *Death of a Salesman*, by Arthur Miller, is also an impelling tragedy but it involves events unimportant to all but the main character, Willy Loman, an unimportant person. The original Broadway setting by Jo Mielziner conveyed a sense of space appropriate to the magnitude of Willy's tragedy; it recreated the small, confining rooms of Willy's house.

Once the concept of size is established, the style of the set must be determined. The script might indicate a definite style—Victorian, French Provincial, or Colonial American, for example. But it is the director's prerogative to change that concept. For example, in almost every period of modern theatrical history, directors have experimented with presenting Shakespeare's plays in contemporary settings. Nor does a realistic play require a realistic set. Realism can be suggested by one or two pieces of furniture—perhaps only a table and chair—on a bare stage. In fact, such stark simplicity could have a more powerful effect on the audience than an elaborate set that faithfully reproduces a room. The photographs here show a variety of set styles that range from the most abstract (above, *The Birds*) to the most conventional (page 2215, *The Chalk Garden*).

When the stylistic choices have been made, the designer finally comes to grips with the tangible aspects of the sets. What exits and entrances are required, how many, and of what nature—doors, windows, trapdoors? What must come through them—actors only, or perhaps coffins or baby buggies? Possible costumes are considered; will long flowing robes or wide-hooped skirts fit? Are large props like trunks or wheelchairs indicated? These are major factors in designing the set's

During the seventeenth century, Italian and French stage designers favored elaborate painted backdrops depicting complex architectural structures rendered in accurate perspective drawings. Though visually impressive, they were impossibly distracting and overwhelmed the performers, who were often lost in the dizzying detail.

A model for an imagined set for a children's operetta based on *Winnie the Pooh* is constructed of artist's foam board and drawing paper, and is painted with watercolors. Such models, built to scale, give a set designer a good idea of how his ideas will look and work in actual construction.

superstructure. As in building a house, architecture must be determined before interior decoration can begin. But then every choice made—colors, textures, fabrics, decorative trim, fixtures, furniture—must be in harmony with the style established jointly by director and designer. The designer is free to make suggestions and add his own ideas to the total picture.

Rendering the Stage Picture

Guided by his notes and conversations, the designer sketches his impression of each scene in the play, sometimes sketching the same scene in different lights or times of day. He may use pencil, ink, or watercolor. He takes into account the actual stage space available. A proscenium theater poses the fewest set-design problems, since the audience views the action from the front at all times. In effect, the stage pictured is designed in a box from which one side (called the fourth wall) has been removed.

Set sketches do not contain minute detail, but they do suggest the colors, style, and overall feeling the designer wishes to convey. When he has sketched his impression of each scene, he shows the drawings to the director, and they compare impressions. Are the colors, moods, and visual relationships right? Are spaces large enough to accommodate the action? They also study details. If the set is realistic, are the doors and windows in the right places for the way the play will be staged? If there is conventional furniture, is it the right style? This is the time when any differences between the set designer and the director are reconciled. Cooperation and compromise are essential if the collaboration is to be successful.

The final set of designer renderings incorporates all changes that have been approved by the director. At this point, the designer may make a scale model of the set, though this is optional. If the set if complicated, a scale model helps show what the scenery will look like in three dimensions. The model also helps in working out mechanical problems that will arise in building the scenery. In the photograph at top left, a scale model of a set for an imaginary children's operetta, based on the story of *Winnie the Pooh*, is shown. Though not designed for a specific theater or an actual production, the model shows the basic structure of a set using simple painted flats (see Craftnotes, page 2202) to create an outdoor-indoor scene, and demonstrates the major work in constructing such a set: the building and painting of flats.

Ground Plan

Even if a scale model is not needed, the designer must draw a floor plan of the stage with the scenery in place. This is called a ground plan. It is a view of the set from above, drawn to scale like a house plan. It is necessary to relate the various scenic elements to the actual stage.

To draw an accurate ground plan, the designer first must measure the entire stage and draw it in scale, with all of its architectural features—walls, doors, proscenium arch (where the stage ends in relation to the audience) and so forth. After he determines the size and placement of each element of the set—such as walls, raised platforms, stairs, or furniture—the designer indicates each placement on the ground plan. Several ground plans are shown in the figures that accompany the renderings of working sets on other pages. A separate ground plan is made for each scene in which the setting changes.

In most productions, rehearsals for the play will have begun by this point. For the benefit of the actors, the designer may be asked to indicate where the set will project onto the stage. Walls and areas that will be covered by platforms may be outlined with masking tape on the stage floor. Tables and chairs may be indicated temporarily by milk crates and folding chairs.

Set Construction

The designer divides the setting into separate scenic elements that must be built—wall sections, doors, windows, stairs, platforms, and the like. He draws each piece to scale, including accurate dimensions for the length, width, and height.

Many sets, whether realistic or abstract, call for the construction of walls. The basic unit of wall construction in the theater is called a flat (see Craftnotes, page 2202). A flat is a wood frame over which canvas is stretched and tacked. Flats are light, easily moved modules which can be painted with any design. In the set for

The Chalk Garden (page 2215), flats create a realistic drawing-room setting. They also create the exterior walls in the set for *Picnic* (page 2210). Flats can incorporate doors and windows, and when used with platforms, can help the designer achieve multilevel, three-dimensional effects. The sizes given for flats in the Craftnotes (page 2202) are average, based on the actual height of normal room ceilings; those for the platforms are based on the stock sizes of plywood sheets. Flats can be built as high as 18 feet if necessary. Platforms can be raised by bolting on legs of 2-by-4 lumber, and they can be contoured by cutting the plywood into any desired shape. The setting for *The Birds* (page 2197) consists almost entirely of platforms of varying heights, massed together to suggest a mountaintop.

Drops, Wings, and Borders

A drop is a piece of cloth—usually canvas—that hangs from a rod, called a batten, at the sides or back of the stage. The canvas is weighted at the bottom but hangs free and is usually painted with a representative scene. When a drop forms the entire back of a set from top to bottom and side to side, it is called a backdrop. Narrower drops are often used at the sides of a stage in conjunction with a backdrop. These are called wings, or legs, and can be soft—made of canvas and hung—or hard—made like a flat or from a piece of insulation board. A narrow drop hung horizontally across the top of the stage is the border. A set built in this manner is called a wing-and-border set, a style that was very popular at the turn of the century. Scenes from a production of the W. S. Gilbert play, *Engaged*, with sets in this style, are shown on pages 2200 and 2201. Following a traditional practice, the front curtain is a drop painted like a billboard with the name of the play.

In many proscenium theaters, the stage house—the area surrounding the stage, above, below, and at the sides—includes a high loft area above the stage called the flies. Scenery such as drops may be raised (flown) out of sight. Wing-and-border sets that call for many changes of scene are ideally performed in theaters where the drops can be raised and lowered easily.

Cycloramas

It is often necessary to create a smooth surface encircling the back and sides of a stage, so it can be lit to represent sky or limitless space. This is true of the sets for *The Birds* (page 2197), *Picnic* (page 2210), *Young Ben Franklin* (page 2208), and *The Chalk Garden* (page 2215). This scenic element is cyclorama, or cyc, and is usually made of cotton duck, stretched smoothly between curved battens at top and bottom. Such a batten is indicated in the ground plan for *The Birds* (page 2197). A cyc can also be made with three flat drops that abut at wide angles. A very wide, continuously curved cyc requires careful seaming and must be stretched as free of wrinkles as possible. A gauze drop, called a scrim, is usually hung directly in front of the cyc to mask the seams and wrinkles. Since a cyclorama is rarely painted anything but a neutral gray, it offers the lighting designer a canvas on which to create any number of effects with colored light, light patterns, or projections.

Painting Elevations

If the set designer does not do the painting himself, or does not supervise the artist who does, he must prepare painting elevations. These combine carefully scaled drawings with color renderings for each major piece of scenery. A wall section will show precisely what color to paint each area, along with shading, texture, moldings, and any other detailing. Most designers do painting elevations even if they plan to paint the scenery themselves, since it is easy to plan the painting on a small scale and see how it will look when finished. Revisions are easier than on full-sized scenery. The Craftnotes on page 2205 introduce basic scene-painting techniques for achieving specific effects.

Executing the Design

Although wood and canvas held together with glue and nails are the traditional materials used for the construction of scenery, any available material may be substituted—cardboard, plastic, even metal. Professional set designers apply these criteria: They use the most economical material that will do the job. They use the lightest material that is strong enough. And they make sure they have craftsmen with the skills and tools required to handle the material.

Scheduling is the key

Everything in the professional theater hinges on efficient scheduling. The director and the stage manager provide a master schedule and coordinate the activities of all members of the cast and production staff, making sure work dovetails at certain target dates. The most important target is opening night. "The show must go on" is a theatrical tradition taken very seriously. Rarely is an opening canceled or changed due to anything less than a natural disaster. When the director asks for a finished set on a particular date, the designer does everything in his power to honor that date. A typical rehearsal period is six weeks. Usually the major work on a set is finished at least a week before the opening. If the set requires the construction of many large pieces of scenery, time is scheduled accordingly, with the help of specialists if necessary.

The production staff

Professional theater people—be they actors, directors, producers, or designers—are all working toward one goal: the production of a play. To function as a team, each must understand his role and the roles of others. Actors and directors work primarily on words and actions, but the designers and technicians are concerned with physical environment: scenery, costumes, props, lighting, and sound. In the description of a typical production staff on page 2204, you will note that specific responsibilities are given the heads of each department so order can be maintained in what could easily become chaotic. In amateur theater, it is common for one person to fill more than one role. A director, for example, may also act as a scene or lighting designer; actors often double as stage hands and construction workers when they are not rehearsing; the lighting designer may execute cues during the show (see page 2214). Ideally, though, people do the best work when distractions are kept to a minimum.

Wing-and-border settings for a play by W. S. Gilbert, *Engaged*, are shown above and opposite. Popular at the turn of the century, this type of setting is characterized by the use of painted canvas drops hung at the rear and sides of the stage. The title of the play was traditionally painted on the *entracte* curtain, as above, which was just another drop painted to resemble a real curtain. The old-fashioned footlights are simulated.

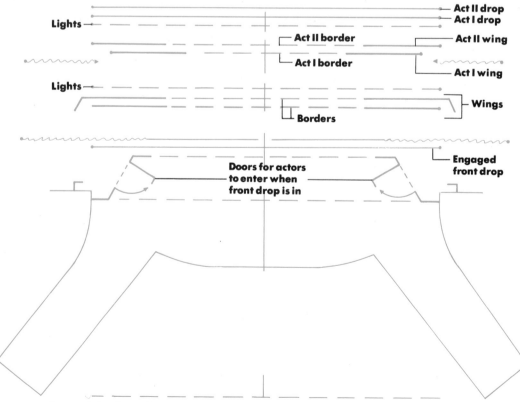

A ground plan shows the arrangement of drops for the *Engaged* set. To change scenery, the drops are raised, or flown, out of sight above the stage, and others are lowered.

A drawing-room scene for *Engaged* is enlivened by a fancifully painted backdrop drawn in comic perspective. Details such as reflections painted on the "mirrors" and furniture drawn in a scale that relates logically to real stage furniture conspire to make the *trompe-l'oeil* a success.

The designer/artist used a full-blown cartoon style to render an outdoor setting for *Engaged*. The bridge at the center, easily mistaken for part of the backdrop, is actually a three-dimensional set piece.

10"

90° angle

¼" plywood

10"

Detail A
Typical corner block

¼" plywood

Detail B
Keystone

Top rail

Diagonal brace

Toggle

Stiles

Bottom rail

9' 0"

4' 6"

For additional support, the flats and jacks can be blocked into the floor, as illustrated. A block of wood such as a short piece of 2-by-4 is nailed to the floor; then the flat or jack is nailed to the block. This keeps the flats from being lifted.

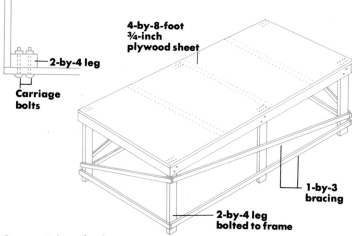

4-by-8-foot ¾-inch plywood sheet

2-by-4 leg

Carriage bolts

1-by-3 bracing

2-by-4 leg bolted to frame

Constructing flats

A flat is typically made of 1-by-3-inch lumber and canvas; the drawing above shows how it is assembled. First, corners of the rectangle of wood boards are nailed together; then the framework is reinforced with two diagonal braces and a crosspiece. Joints are further strengthened with triangles of plywood (detail A) or keystones (detail B). The front of the frame is covered with muslin or canvas, glued and stapled in place.

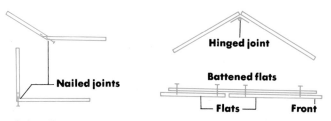

Hinged joint

Nailed joints

Battened flats

Flats

Front

Joining flats

Flats can be assembled in several ways. They can be abutted at right angles and nailed together. If edges are beveled, the flats can be nailed together at an angle.

In an inside corner, flats can be hinged together by screwing leaf hinges to the face of the flats. (The hinges and joint are concealed with a strip of canvas glued over them and painted with the flats.)

If the flats are to be butted edge-to-edge in a straight line, they can be joined with a batten (a 1-by-3 horizontal wood strip will do) nailed or screwed across the back of the joint.

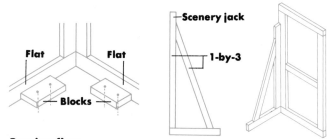

Flat

Flat

Blocks

Scenery jack

1-by-3

Bracing flats

Flats joined at angles will generally hold each other up, as long as weak points and the end flats are supported with scenery jacks (above, center and right). These are braces made of 1-by-3 lumber joined the same way as the flats themselves. A door flat may require extra jacks to prevent movement of the flat when the door is used.

Constructing platforms

A solid-frame platform consists of rectangular framing and a top piece called a lid. The framing can be made from any stock lumber, usually 1 to 2 inches thick and 4 to 12 inches wide. Frame pieces are cut to size and assembled into a rectangle with glued and nailed joints. Reinforcing crosspieces are added every two feet. The lid is ¾-inch-plywood which comes in standard 4-by-8 foot sheets. Platforms are often constructed to these dimensions, although the plywood can be cut to any size or shape. The plywood is then glued and nailed on top of the frame.

Beyond a height of 12 inches, legs are bolted to the platform frame (left, above). For a 4-by-8-foot platform, six legs made of 2-by-4 lumber are generally used. Beyond a height of 18 inches, diagonal bracing of the legs with 1-by-3 lumber makes the platform safer.

Wood platforms can be very noisy. Carpeting the platform helps muffle footsteps. To keep a platform from looking carpeted, canvas can be stretched over the carpeting and painted, or indoor-outdoor carpeting can itself be painted.

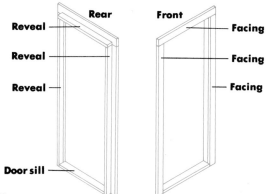

Rear

Front

Reveal

Reveal

Reveal

Facing

Facing

Facing

Door sill

Doors

A door jamb—the frame that holds the door—consists of three facings, three reveals, and one sill (above). The facings are for decoration; they may be curved, or have moldings applied to simulate any architectural style. The reveals—wood strips at right angles to the facings—simulate the thickness of a wall. A door sill is needed to

PLATFORMS, DOORS, AND WINDOWS

hold the unit together if it is to be stored separately from its flat; it should be beveled front and rear to reduce the possibility of someone tripping on it.

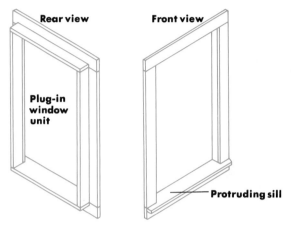

Typical door flat

Corner block

9'0"

Keystone

Muslin or canvas

1-by-3 clear white pine

Rear view

Opening for plug-in door unit

6'4"

Allow ¼" clearance to insert door unit

3'6"

1'3" — 2'6" — 1'3"
5'0"

If the door jamb is built into a flat, rather than between two flats, then the door sill may be eliminated. In this case, an alternate method of construction is sometimes used, with the frame of the flat sandwiched between the facings and the reveals of the jamb.

Plywood or hardboard

Plan view of door

Simple stage door

Door opens onstage

Reveal

Jambs

¾-by-¾-inch door stops

Reveal

Door opens offstage

The door jamb is built of stock lumber (generally pine) in sizes of 1-by-3, 1-by-4, 1-by-6, or whatever size the designer specifies.

Stock interior doors (hollow-core doors are lightest and least expensive) are available at most lumberyards. They have plain surfaces but molding or other decoration can be added. Doors can also be built of ⅛-inch- or ¼-inch-thick hardboard or plywood, framed as shown above, left.

Passage door knobs (made for interior doors) are used in most stage settings. They come with installation instructions.

The door stops illustrated are ¾-by-¾-inch strips installed after the door is hinged to the jamb. The stops prevent the door from swinging past its closed position. Butt hinges are generally used to hang the door—two or three of an appropriate size, depending on the thickness of the door used.

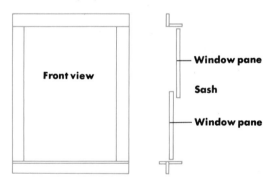

Rear view

Front view

Plug-in window unit

Protruding sill

Windows

A window frame is made much the same as a door jamb. Both are fitted into an opening in a door or window flat. Often, for architectural realism, the windowsill projects into the room.

Front view

Window pane

Sash

Window pane

The same type of frame can be used for a sash window (the kind that slides up and down) or a casement window (hinged like a door). A sash window requires guides—small strips of wood—attached to the surfaces of the reveals to create channels that keep the window in place as it slides up and down.

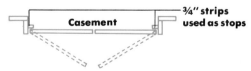

Casement

¾" strips used as stops

The casement window, hinged like a door, needs stops to keep it from closing too far.

You can make either type of window from 1-by-2 or 1-by-3 wood strips for the sash frames and ¾-by-¾-inch strips for the mullions (divisions between panes). Real glass is almost never used. Substitutes include plastic and various sheer fabrics such as gauze or bobbinet, which look surprisingly like glass. Ordinary window screening is sometimes used.

PROFESSIONALS THE AUDIENCE NEVER SEES

Management

The director
Primarily responsible for the dramatic presentation of the play, the director is usually the one to choose the script and cast the show. He conducts all rehearsals, coaches the actors in their lines, and choreographs their movements on stage (this is called blocking).

The production stage manager
The production stage manager is the director's top assistant. He schedules auditions and rehearsals, keeps the prompt book (a copy of the script with the director's notes) and all production notes, and is responsible for backstage discipline and organization during rehearsal and performance.

The house manager
The house manager is responsible for keeping order in the front of the house, (i.e. the box office and auditorium) coordinating the ushers, timing the intermissions, and alerting the actors backstage when the show is about to begin, at the outset and after each intermission.

Designers
The set designer is responsible for the visual aspects of scenery and props. He makes preliminary color sketches and final renderings of the scenery, as well as technical drawings showing how the scenery is to be built and how any moving part will work. In the absence of a scenic artist, the designer also paints the scenery.

The lighting designer is responsible for planning the lighting, specifying the equipment necessary to execute the design, focusing the lights, and arranging (with the stage manager) when lighting cues will occur.

The costume designer is responsible for planning the costumes by sketching them in color and selecting the materials from which each costume will be made. The costume designer then supervises the construction and fitting of each costume.

Technical staff
The technical director heads the technical staff and coordinates its efforts, acting as liaison with designers, stage manager, and director.

The master carpenter heads a crew of carpenters who construct and assemble the scenery, install it in the theater, and maintain it in good condition. The carpentry crew also changes the scenery as necessary for each scene during the show.

The master electrician heads a crew of electricians who set up and operate all lighting equipment; this includes changes during a performance.

The properties master stores and maintains all hand props (small objects used by actors on stage) and makes them available to the actors at the proper time during a performance.

The wardrobe mistress stores, maintains, and cleans costumes and, if necessary, provides assistance in dressing and changing.

TYPES OF THEATERS

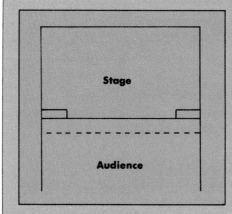

The proscenium theater
This type of theater takes its name from the proscenium, the arch in the fourth side of the stage through which the audience views the production. The action of the play generally takes place behind the proscenium (upstage), so a curtain can be used to cut off the audience's view between scenes. A number of sets of scenery can be used in a single show, with changes taking place when the curtain is down. Lighting for this type of theater is described on pages 2208 through 2215.

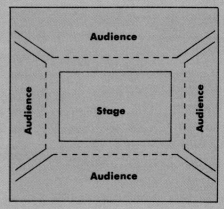

The extended apron or thrust stage
The part of the stage in a proscenium theater nearest the audience is called the apron (downstage). When it projects into the audience seating area, an extended apron or thrust stage is created. In this type of theater, the action of the play may take place both upstage and downstage from the proscenium arch, or exclusively in front of it, depending on the production. The lighting remains basically the same as for a proscenium stage. But there is no curtain to mask scenery changes in front of the arch, so either the scenery is not changed there or it is kept portable enough so that it can be changed quickly in view of the audience.

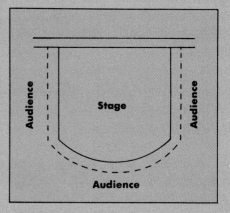

The three-sided arena
When the apron of the stage is extended so far into the audience that the side seats must face in toward the stage, a three-sided arena results. The area upstage from the proscenium (behind the curtain) then becomes unusable, since part of the audience could not see it. Scenery in this type of theater is affected the same way as on the extended-apron stage. Since the audience surrounds the stage on three sides, it is necessary to have light coming from three sides. Downlighting is unaffected but sidelighting is difficult to handle, since different parts of the audience get vastly different views of the stage.

The full arena
When the audience completely surrounds a stage on all sides, as in most circus performances, a full-arena stage results. Scenery on this type of stage must be minimal, very light, and open, so the audience view of the stage is not obstructed from any angle. Any scenery change takes place in view of the audience, and the pieces must be carried up aisles through the audience. Lighting is even more difficult than in the three-sided arena. General illumination from all sides is heavily used.

CRAFTNOTES: SCENE PAINTING TECHNIQUES

Paint used by scenic artists consists of three elements—pigment to give it color; a medium, usually oil or water, to carry the pigment; and a binder to hold the pigment together when the base medium dries. Paints differ according to the base medium and the type of binder used. Casein, a premixed water-based paint (it can be cleaned up with soap and water) is the type most widely used on scenery. Colors can be mixed to obtain other colors or shades; but when a special color is needed, enough should be mixed to finish the job; it is difficult to match a special color later.

Dry brush
Strokes like those illustrated above, called dry-brush strokes, are created by using a small amount of paint on a dry brush (not previously dipped or wetted). Scenic artists save old worn-out brushes for this purpose. The matted bristles give a desired streaked effect.

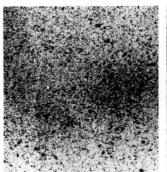

Dribble and spatter
Paint may be dribbled and spattered on a surface to create various effects. A large dribble (above, right) is often used on a painted floor to relieve the flatness of the large paint area. The spatter can be created with a spray gun or by hitting the brush-holding hand against the other arm, causing paint to fly off the brush in drops. A small spatter (above, left) can be used to tone, soften, or highlight an undercoat. It is used as the final step in both marbleizing and wood-graining (page 2207).

Application
The three types of brushes used most often for scene painting are base-coat brushes, 8 inches wide; layout brushes, 2 to 6 inches wide; and lining brushes, 1 to 2 inches wide. Rollers or spray guns can take the place of base-coat brushes for large areas, but not for details. Most paints need to be thinned and strained for spray application.

Scenic artists have developed many techniques for creating special effects with paint. For example, brush strokes can be made with the broad side of a lining brush, the thin side of the lining brush, or the tip of the lining brush (see the top three strokes, above). As the brush begins to run dry, broken lines result, as shown in the balance of the strokes above.

Wash

A wash of color implies a color gradation from dark to light. Such a wash is usually applied on a large wall surface, using paint in three tones of the same color, one dark, one medium, and one very light, as in the color samples above. The surface to be painted must be flat on the floor to avoid runs. If the area is extremely large, the artist may attach his brush to a long bamboo pole and paint standing up. The paint used must be watery and in addition a bucket of water is kept nearby so lines can be further blended, keeping the wash gradual and subtle.

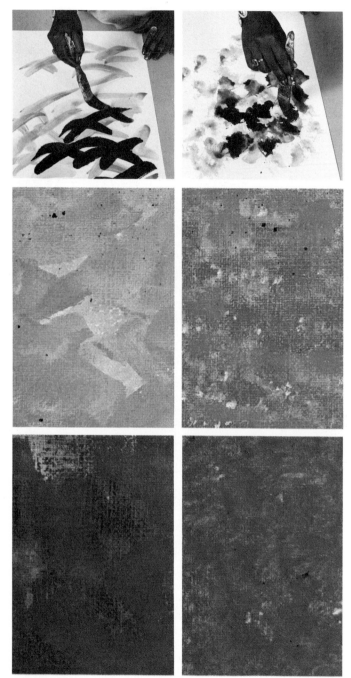

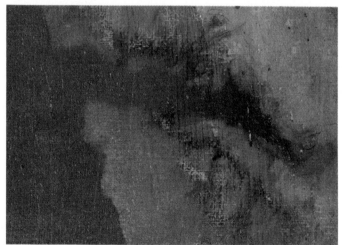

Wet blend

The wet blend effect, illustrated above, is achieved with a technique used to fuse several colors. It is used to break up the starkness of one color, to achieve texture (as an alternate to the marbleizing technique shown opposite), and to create a weathered look. To wet blend, the artist wets the canvas slightly at first, then uses watery paint and a brush to apply any colors he wishes. Water is sometimes spattered on the wet paint to make it run.

Scumbling

Scumbling is a method of applying two colors of paint almost simultaneously so they meld but do not totally blend. This may be done in the two ways shown in the photographs above. At left, the colors are being applied by the artist on a dry canvas with the broad side of a lining brush using back-and-forth strokes. The paint is of a medium consistency, neither thick nor thin. This method has been used on the samples above, left, where the brush strokes are most evident. At right, above, the scenic artist applies the paint by bouncing the tip of the brush down on the surface to be painted. This creates the effect shown in the color samples at the right, above.

PAINTING TECHNIQUES

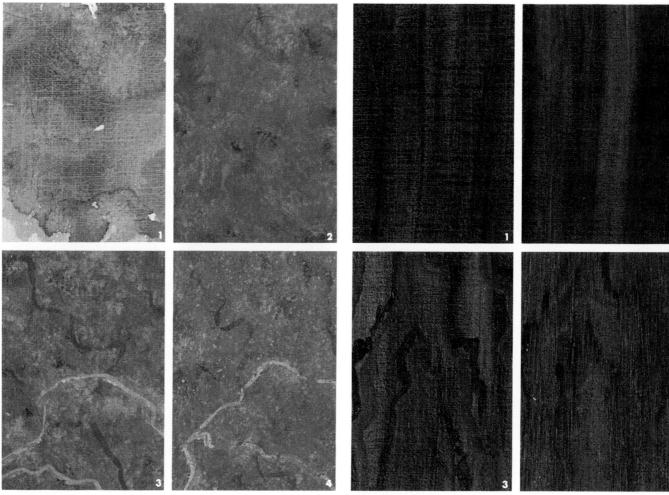

Marbleizing

A marbleized effect is achieved in four steps. In the example shown above, the basic color is medium blue, and three other shades of blue are used in successively grayer tones. These colors were first sponged thickly onto the surface over each other to achieve a mottled effect without brush strokes (1). When this surface had dried, subtly contrasting colors, ocher and brown, were sponged over the blue to create highlights (2).

When all of the sponged-in color had dried, the veining was applied with a thin brush and a watery mixture of the lightest blue and white for the light veining and, in this case, purple for the darker veining (3). Crisscrossing the two colors of veining and varying the thickness of the lines simulate the veining of real marble. In the final marbleizing step (4), the same watery light paint used for veining was used to spatter the entire surface. This helps to diffuse the color. As a final finishing step, when the paint is dry, the marbleized surface can be protected with clear vinyl latex paint in a matte (flat) finish or, if preferred, a glossy finish (for a polished look).

Wood graining

Two browns close in color can be used to simulate wood grain. In the example above, a red-brown and gray-brown were used. Brush on first one, then the other, using straight parallel brush strokes (1).

Streak the paint at intervals with a damp or nearly dry brush while the paint is still wet (2).

Mix a deeper and a lighter tone of one of the original colors (darken with a darker brown and lighten with white). Make this paint watery and grain the wood with a thin brush, varying the lines (3).

While this paint is still wet, streak upwards with a very dry brush, preferably a worn brush with missing bristles (4). This completes the wood graining. As with marbleizing, the finished surface can be painted with clear vinyl latex paint in matte or glossy finish.

In this cutout profile set for *Young Ben Franklin*, a children's play, a nonrealistic interior floats against a cyclorama background (page 2199) lighted to suggest space that could be anywhere and anytime.

Performing Arts
Stage lighting

For practical as well as artistic reasons, theatrical productions depend heavily on lighting. A professional play may require more than 100 lights, miles of cable, and an array of sophisticated control devices—adding up to tons of equipment, not to mention the technicians needed to operate the system.

Stage lighting is a technical necessity. Most productions take place indoors, after dark, or both, and therefore require artificial light. Shows could be lit like sports events, with enough plain white light to illuminate the action. But as long as light is needed for visibility, it might just as well be used artistically. Stage lighting performs a variety of functions, each capable of enhancing the performance as a work of art. But it is impossible to be a lighting artist without first being a competent lighting technician. Whether the lighting designer works with ten light sources or 1,000, he needs an understanding of the nature of light—how it is produced artificially, and how it can be controlled.

The Nature of Light

Stage lighting imitates nature. There are two kinds of natural light—general indirect light, as from an overcast sky or reflected sunlight, and specific direct light, such as direct sunlight on a cloudless day. Indirect light will cast a hazy shadow or none at all; direct light will cast a sharp-edged shadow. Artificially produced light can also be direct or indirect, but in either case, it possesses four other characteristics of light—intensity, color, distribution, and movement. When light is produced artificially, these characteristics can be controlled.

Intensity or Brightness

The human eye can accept a wide range of brightness, from the light of a single candle to hundreds of times that much. The intensity of light in a theater depends upon the number of light sources, their output, their distance from the stage, and the level at which the dimmers are set (see Control of Stage Lights, page 2212).

The intensity of light used has the ability to suggest a mood to the audience. Unless other factors are present, bright light will make an audience more alert and more disposed to feel cheerful, but dim light, which is fatiguing, will have a depressing effect. (This happens in nature, too.)

Any color filter used with a light source will reduce its brightness as well as change its color. Contrast between the brightness on different parts of the stage, or

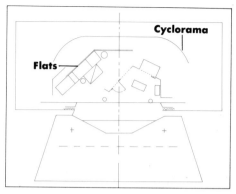

The simplicity of this set design is evident in the ground plan. The curved cyclorama is at the rear. A simple arrangement of flats, hinged to form angles, creates the interior of the print shop.

A dramatic silhouette of the set opposite is achieved when the lighting technician turns off all set lights except for those that wash over the cyclorama.

with the brightness of a previous scene, intensifies the effect of the light. The color and texture of the surfaces on which light falls affect its apparent brightness; dark colored or heavily textured scenery, costumes, or makeup reflect less light and appear darker on stage than light-colored or smooth and shiny items. It takes time for the eye to adapt to changing levels of light. The greater the difference in brightness, the longer this adjustment will take.

Color

The color that any object appears to be is a product of its actual color and the color of the light by which it is viewed. Natural light is usually white light, made up of all visible hues. But in the theater, the color of each light source can be controlled by using filters to block all but the desired color. These filters are made from three materials: gelatin, the cheapest, fades easily; plastic, which is more expensive, is more durable; glass, the most expensive, will never fade. These materials are fitted into frames that attach in front of the lights.

Color in stage lighting can be used to modify the colors of makeup, scenery, or costumes. For example, any color will appear deeper and more vibrant when seen by light of the same color. A white object will take on the color of whatever light is directed toward it. But when an object is viewed by light of a color complementary to itself (as a blue-green object seen by red light) the two colors tend to cancel each other and the object appears dark gray or black.

Color in light can affect mood in much the same way, and for similar reasons, as intensity. The warmer colors (pinks, reds, ambers, and yellows) seem to suggest cheer, perhaps because they are associated with fair weather. They are used extensively to light comedies. The cooler colors (blues and violets) seem to suggest a somber mood (when someone is unhappy, he is said to have the blues). These colors find a wider use in lighting serious or tragic drama.

However, warm and cool qualities of color in light are relative. They are affected by other colors on stage at the same time and by colors seen previously. Lavender light, for example, will seem cool compared with amber, but it will seem warm when viewed next to or immediately after steel blue.

Distribution

The term, distribution, encompasses both the direction from which light comes and the form it takes. A light source can be placed in an endless number of possible positions to vary the direction from which light comes (see Craftnotes, pages 2214 and 2215). Light can take different shapes as it leaves its source. If the beam is relatively narrow, the light is called a spot; if it is quite wide, it is called a flood.

A naturalistic front-porch setting for *Picnic* by William Inge calls for natural lighting effects. Light on the cyclorama at the rear is used to indicate the time of day—morning in the photograph above—and to convey a summertime mood.

Spotlights throw hard, sharp beams of light with clearly defined edges. Anything in a spotlight will have a dark, sharp-edged shadow. A floodlight casts a more diffuse beam of light, one that falls off gradually in intensity towards its edges. An object in a floodlight will have a fuzzy, indistinct shadow. In any one scene, light may come from several directions and from a combination of spots and floods.

Movement
Any change in the intensity, color, or distribution of stage lighting is called movement. Any one of these properties can be altered singly or in conjunction with any other. Color may be changed by fading out one set of lights with, say, red filters and bringing up another set with blue. Intensity may be changed by varying the dimmer readings. Distribution may be altered by switching from one set of light source to another.

If a lighting designer wanted to create a sunset effect, for example, he might use the following movement: He would decrease the intensity of the light, he would make the color gradually deeper and warmer, and he would lower the angle of light and make it more diffuse to simulate the disappearance of the direct light source, the sun, followed by reflected light for the sky.

Stage-Lighting Objectives
Selective visibility: The lighting designer's most important job is to illuminate those areas and objects on stage that the audience should see. Each must be given the proper amount of light. Whatever is unimportant may be left dark or dimly lighted. The visibility of an object depends on the amount of light aimed at it, but visibility is also relative. An object with only a little light on it will be visible if the rest of the stage is dark. If the amount of light on the object remains unchanged but the rest of the stage becomes brighter, the original object will become less visible. The eye is always attracted to the brightest object in its field of vision.

When the balance of visibility is changed, the lighting designer indicates to the audience where it should direct its attention. A spotlight that follows a performer

When viewed together, the photographs opposite and above illustrate movement in stage light. In the transition from morning light (opposite) to late afternoon light (above), the angle, color, and intensity of the light are altered, changing the mood of the scene.

around the stage is an obvious cue, while a stationary slow fade is a subtle one (as the intensity of light is increased or decreased, the light is said to fade up or fade down). Selective visibility on stage functions much like a close-up in film or television. It focuses audience attention on a detail of the total picture.

Plausibility: The lighting must be kept plausible in terms of the settings, costumes, time, place, and action of the play. If the production is realistic, for example, the sunlight must look like sunlight. Even if the style is not totally realistic, the lighting must seem possible in terms of whatever reality is established. If the lighting is at odds with the action (too bright when it should be night, too warm when it should be winter) the audience will be confused by the conflicting indications as to what they should feel about what they see and hear.

Revelation of form: "Shade and shadow are equal in importance to light itself," said Adolphe Appia, one of the most innovative stage designers of this century. General, diffuse floodlight illumination, while providing plenty of visibility, often makes three-dimensional objects look flat and featureless because hard shadows are absent. To reveal form with shadow, a lighting designer uses tightly controlled spotlighting, often from extreme angles at the sides and back as well as the front.

Composition: Composition is achieved by using color and intensity appropriately in relation to the theme of the play, and by making the various visual elements on stage selectively visible while revealing their three-dimensional form. The sets, costumes, and props compose a picture on the stage, but the lighting must reveal and highlight details of the composition.

Mood: Mood is the result of using light to achieve the preceding objectives. If each is met as the stage picture is composed, the mood of the drama will be enhanced by the lighting.

The last two objectives, mood and composition, grow out of the first three, selective visibility, plausibility, and revelation of form. A lighting designer does not start by trying to create either mood or a pretty stage picture. Visibility is always the most important element in his design.

Some electricity basics

Electricity is the flow of electrons through a conductor. Conductors are materials that permit the passage of an electric current. Silver is the best conductor, but it is too costly for general use. Copper is the most practical. Brass and aluminum also have limited use.

Insulators are materials that block the passage of an electric current. Unbroken insulators are essential since many substances (including the human body) have some degree of conductivity. Some rigid insulating materials for permanent installations are glass, ceramic, and slate. Some flexible ones for wire and cables are rubber, fiber asbestos, and various types of vinyls and other plastics.

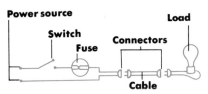

Components of simple electric circuits

Wire or cable consists of stranded copper conductors, insulated usually with a rubber jacket, having connectors at both ends. Plugs and sockets are familiar home connectors.

Connectors are used rather than permanent attachments because of the temporary nature of stage lighting. Common types of connectors used in a theater are the stage plug, the pin connector, the twist lock, and the parallel blade.

Switches are mechanical devices used to open and close electrical circuits. An open circuit (one that does not provide a continuous path for the current) will not permit the current to flow or any equipment on that circuit to operate. A closed circuit does allow current to flow.

A dimmer is a special type of switch which can vary the amount of current flow. It may be set to allow the passage of any part of the full current available. A light on the dimmer may be set at any brightness up to its maximum.

Fuses and circuit breakers are devices used to protect wiring, equipment, and people by automatically opening a circuit in case of a short ciruit or an overloaded circuit that otherwise might start a fire. A fuse is an intentionally weak link meant to burn out first, before any other equipment on the circuit is damaged. A burned-out fuse must be replaced after the short or overload that caused the burnout is corrected. A circuit breaker is a switch that opens the circuit automatically when it is overloaded. These devices can be reset easily, but this must never be done until the cause of the overload is found and corrected.

The power source for theater and home use is usually the local electric company generator, which is connected to the wall outlets into which lamps and appliances are plugged.

The load is determined by whatever pieces of electrical equipment are being operated on a circuit at one time.

Specials

Specific places on stage often require special lighting. In theater jargon, any such light is called a special. Doorways always seem to need a special because they are at the very edge of the area visible to the audience and are often important because the entrances of actors are important. Similarly, any place where an actor sits needs a special so his face remains lit whether he is standing or sitting. An elevated level or staircase requires special lighting for the same reason. A special may also be used wherever a tightly controlled light is required.

Special effects include such things as psychedelic lighting (deep, saturated colors, flashing lights, and quickly changing colors); fire and flame effects; and the illusion of ghosts, clouds, lightning, or explosions. Such effects require skill and precision, but they are not allowed to detract from the primary goal of lighting each actor well.

Film projection is coming into more common use. Every type of projector, from home models to projectors that use 6-inch-square slides, have theatrical applications. Images can be projected onto any part of the set, including the actors.

Control of Stage Lights

Stage lights, which may number anywhere from a dozen to several hundred, are controlled from one or more dimmer boards. A dimmer is a type of switch which can not only turn a light on and off but set it at any brightness level in between. Ideally, there would be one dimmer for each light, but the expense of this is so great that groups of lights are usually ganged together on one dimmer switch. The dimmer board is sometimes permanently installed in a theater, but more often is set up to suit the special needs of a given production. The dimmer board is connected with a special service entrance, similar except in size to a fuse box in a house. The board is also connected by heavy cable with each lighting instrument, the way an extension cord is used to connect a reading lamp with a home outlet.

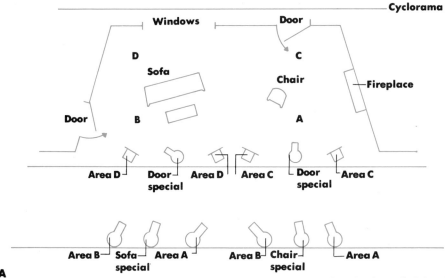

A

Figure A: A ground plan that includes the location of lighting instruments for a simple, realistic interior set is shown above. Included are lamps for area lighting and specials for furniture and doors.

A Standard Method of Stage Lighting

The following method of stage lighting, with infinite variations, is used by many professional designers. It is generally attributed to Stanley McCandless, a pioneer of lighting design in the American theater.

Lighting the Acting Area

The first and most important step is to light the acting area. This area is divided into sections of a size that can be covered with a single spotlight beam, usually 6 to 10 feet in diameter (Figure A). Each of these areas is lighted from two spotlight sources, one placed on each side above and to the front. Forty-five degrees above and to each side is considered ideal, but there is a good deal of leeway in this formula. Because these two lights may tend to wash out each other's form-revealing shadows, two colors, one warm and the other cool, may be used to differentiate the light from the two sources. The eye will interpret cool light as shadow; yet the shadow area will be well lit. The colors should be pale so they do not distort the actors' natural skin tones. These pairs of lights satisfy the basic requirement of visibility on stage. Other angles may be used to add plasticity to the lighting.

Lighting the Supplementary Areas
In the same manner as for the general acting areas, two sources are used to cover any part of the stage not already lighted (in alcoves, behind arches, on elevated levels, and the like).

Blending and Toning
When it is difficult to light the acting area smoothly with spotlights, the lighting designer uses floodlights to blend the lighting together. This essentially shadowless light fills in gaps or irregularities, without losing the selective quality of spotlighting. These same instruments provide, at the same time, an even tone for the entire stage.

Lighting the Scenery
Surprisingly, the scenery usually is not specifically lighted. If the acting areas are adequately lit, sufficient light will be reflected to light the scenery as well.

Motivating Light
Any light source actually on the stage is called a motivating light. These include candles, oil lamps, electric fixtures, and fires in fireplaces. These sources, visible to the audience, are so called because they motivate the next step.

Motivated Light
Since a motivating light source on the stage, such as a reading lamp, cannot possibly provide enough light to look real, it is necessary to focus spotlights on the area around the light, making it bright enough to create the illusion that the lamp is indeed lighting the area. It sometimes is possible to use the lights for one of the acting areas at a brighter level to achieve this effect.

Designing the Lighting
The lighting designer must study the play, just as a set designer does, and note its lighting requirements. He must be aware of times of day, season of the year, presence or absence of windows (for daylight or sunlight), any presence of lamps or chandeliers in the setting. He notes blackouts and special effects required, such as fireplaces or sunsets. The mood of the play will have a direct bearing on his lighting.

He then consults with the director to learn his concepts for general lighting. Should it be bright or dim, warm or cool? Will the lighting be soft and shadowless, or harsh and sharp with deep, dramatic shadows? Then he discusses the specific requirements of the play. Will the director follow the script, or will he eliminate some of the indicated requirements and add others? What areas will be used most by the actors? Where will it be important to focus attention with light?

When all of these questions have been answered, the lighting designer attends a run-through rehearsal of the entire play. He notes how the action of the play affects how lighting must be used. What areas actually are most used by the actors? If all the action in a given scene is in one area, is that the only area that needs light, or should the rest of the set be lighted as well? He notes where the director has planned certain changes in lighting, as by having an actor flip on a light switch or open a curtain to admit light.

With all these specifics in mind, he is ready to plan the lighting design. He draws a floor plan of the theater to scale, complete with scenery and positions for hanging lights (Figure A). He draws in symbols representing the types of lighting instruments he wishes to use, in the positions he wishes to place them. He indicates the wattages required in the lamps. He decides the specific color he wants in each light and indicates that on the plan. He indicates the purpose of each light, and which instruments will be controlled by which dimmers. Then he must calculate load capacities to make sure no part of the system is overloaded.

For further reading
Designing for the Theatre: A Memoir and a Portfolio by Jo Mielziner. Atheneum, New York.

The Dramatic Imagination by Robert Edmond Jones. Theater Arts, New York.

G.T.E. Sylvania Lighting Handbook for Television, Theatre, Professional Photography. G.T.E. Sylvania Lighting Center, Danvers, Mass.

A Method of Lighting the Stage by S.R. McCandless. Theater Arts, New York.

Scene Design and Stage Lighting by W. Oren Parker and Harvey K. Smith. Holt, Rinehart and Winston, New York.

Scenery for the Theater by Harold Burris-Meyer and Edward C. Cole. Little, Brown, Boston.

Scenery Then and Now by Donald Oenslager. Norton, New York.

Simon's Directory of Theatrical Materials, Services and Information by Bernard Simon. Package Publicity Service, New York.

Stage Lighting by Richard Pilbrow. Van Nostrand Reinhold, New York.

Theaters and Auditoriums by Harold Burris-Meyer and Edward C. Cole. Van Nostrand Reinhold, New York.

Theatre Books in Print by A.E. Santaniello. Drama Book Shop, New York.

Executing the Design

The electrician who executes the lighting design requires all of this information on the plan in order to set up the required equipment properly. After he installs the necessary lighting instruments, the lighting designer personally supervises the electrician as he focuses each instrument.

After focusing is completed, there is a special lighting rehearsal to decide when lighting changes occur. Changes are signaled—or cued—by spoken words, movement, or sound on stage. Confusingly, the term cue is also used to describe the actual change as it is executed by the lighting technician, so the word has two meanings. For example, a typical first cue in any production would be a signal from the house manager to the lighting technician to bring down the house lights. This cue is then executed, usually slowly, as to a count of five. The next cue, following immediately, is to bring up the lights on the first scene. On a proscenium stage with a curtain, the technician must bring up the stage lights without actually seeing the stage. This he can easily do because all light levels are preset.

Ideally, the stage manager continues to supervise the lighting technician during the performance by calling each cue. This is facilitated by the use of a cue sheet which includes an advance warning, the actual cue (signal) from the stage, and a description of the cue (action) to be executed. Often, in a small production, the lighting technician must follow his own cue sheet, paying close attention to the action on the stage. This requires a complete understanding of the dimmer board, a cool head, and a feeling for the shape, texture, and movement of light.

For related entries see "Costumes," "Masks," and "Skin Painting."

CRAFTNOTES: LIGHTING THE

The basis of drama is the human situation; so the human form is the most interesting and most important visual element on the stage. The face is the most expressive part of that body, and the part that best expresses moods and reveals the moods of others. An audience, viewing a stage, will focus attention on the actor's face first. It is essential that the actor's face be well lighted. The lighting designer can aid the actor in conveying a mood to the audience by lighting his face appropriately. Photographs and drawings on this page show some basic lighting angles. The photographs show the effect of the light from the audience's viewpoint. The illustrations show the position of the lighting instrument relative to the actor facing the audience.

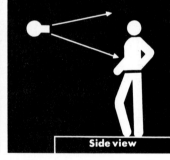

Light coming from the front at eye level flattens and washes out the facial features, giving them no separation from the background. This angle has no dramatic value alone, but it can be used to fill in shadows caused by other lights.

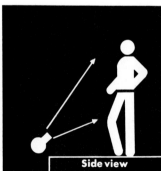

Light coming from the front and below casts shadows upwards. The effect is unnatural, but good for special effects. Footlights in this position are used to tone and blend the general illumination and to soften shadows from the lights above.

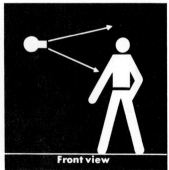

Light coming from the side at a low level gives a very dramatic effect, but one that creates shadow problems. This can be minimized by positioning the lighting instrument above head height, but positioning it below head height can be very effective in dance lighting.

Light is but one of many elements that goes into the creation of a realistic setting like the one above for *The Chalk Garden* by Enid Bagnold. Architectural detail, furnishings, props, doors that open and close, windows through which another scene is suggested, and of course the actors themselves, all contribute to the grand illusion that spells theater.

HUMAN FACE FROM VARIOUS ANGLES

 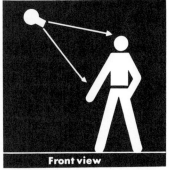

Light coming from the side at a high level gives much of the dramatic effect of low side light, but less of the shadow problem.

 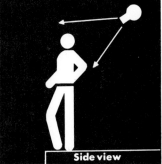

Light from the back and above—sometimes called rim lighting—creates a halo effect which separates the actor from his visual background. It is used in film and television for this purpose.

 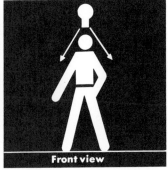

Light coming from directly above creates very deep, dramatic shadows. It has no general illumination value and can be used only as a special effect.

 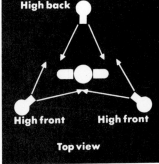

A combination of lights, angled from both sides in front and from the back, generally reveals the form of the human face most naturally. In effect, this is area lighting with a backlight added. There are an infinite number of possible lighting angles. Any combination of these basic angles may be used, plus any interval between them.

STAINED GLASS
Cascading Colors

Erik Erikson, teacher, designer, and crafts-man, studied stained glass in the United States, England, France, and Germany. He designs architectural stained-glass works for both interiors and exteriors of commercial, church, and residential build-ings, and is the author of Step-by-Step Stained Glass.

To step into the dark interior of a European cathedral is, paradoxically, to enter a world of dazzling light and color. Before your eyes become adjusted to the gloom, you look up—the sunlight is transformed into a cascade of multihued brilliance that sparkles and shimmers before your eyes. Only after you are seated and have been looking at the windows for some time do the colors turn to recognizable forms and figures. You are looking at the great stained-glass windows of the Middle Ages.

These medieval masterpieces came into being in concert with Gothic architec-ture, when engineer-architects created a vast interior space that needed to be illu-minated. That made large openings in the walls logical. Glass was available, but large pieces could not be manufactured, so the glass artisans devised a means of joining small pieces of glass with strips of lead. It is likely that this technique was derived from an older one known as cloisonné, in which enamels of different colors were separated with strips of copper or brass.

Although stained glass is traditionally a church art, for a time it was used in the homes of noblemen and wealthy merchants as well. Toward the end of the nine-teenth century, it was reintroduced into home design.

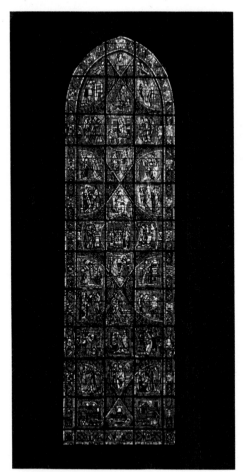

This is one of the 175 stained-glass windows in the Chartres Cathedral in France which were completed between 1200 and 1236. This tremen-dous undertaking brought together glass crafts-men from all over France. Medieval stained-glass windows served as gigantic picture books of Bible stories for congregations unable to read.

It is hard to imagine the variety of effects that can result from using one stained-glass technique. This window was made by Erik Erikson with the same type of lead strips used to join the pieces in the medieval church window at left. Although this is a complex design made of many pieces of glass, the shapes were not difficult to cut.

Another way to use lead in joining colored glass is to make a silhouette panel. This panel, by Erik Erikson, was installed in front of an existing win-dow with brass brackets. The clear glass areas of the design are actually the glass of the window be-hind it. Directions for making a simple leaded stained-glass panel begin on page 2229.

This glass collage filled with subtle, overlapping colors was made by embedding scraps of stained glass in clear liquid epoxy. This is a variation of the glass-lamination technique described on page 2222. Such a collage can be used to make a sparkling sculpture, a hanging panel, a trivet, or simply to brighten an existing window.

A STAINED-GLASS SAMPLER

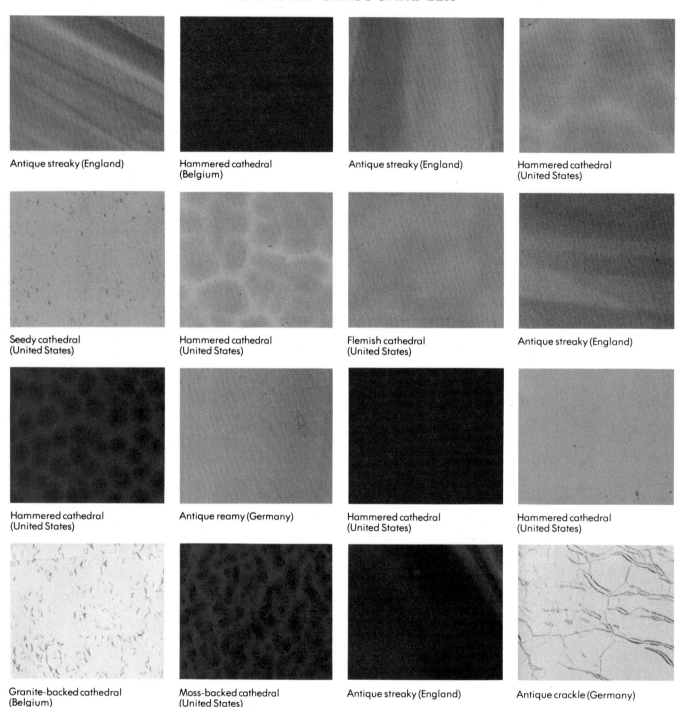

Antique streaky (England)

Hammered cathedral (Belgium)

Antique streaky (England)

Hammered cathedral (United States)

Seedy cathedral (United States)

Hammered cathedral (United States)

Flemish cathedral (United States)

Antique streaky (England)

Hammered cathedral (United States)

Antique reamy (Germany)

Hammered cathedral (United States)

Hammered cathedral (United States)

Granite-backed cathedral (Belgium)

Moss-backed cathedral (United States)

Antique streaky (England)

Antique crackle (Germany)

Shown here is a random sampling of the many types and colors of hand-blown and machine-made glass.

Hand-blown (antique) glass is made by skilled glassblowers and has many air bubbles, waves, and streaks of colors in it. Most antique glass is imported from France, Germany, and England, and is more expensive than the machine-made variety. Streaked glass, called streaky, is usually imported from England, although some originates in Germany. It contains swirls and ripples as well as streaks of delicate colors. Streakies are so beautiful that some stained-glass craftsmen hesitate to cut the glass into design pieces. Another type of antique glass, called crackle glass, is formed by dipping hand-blown glass into water just after it is formed. The shock forms hairline fractures in the glass.

Machine-made glass (called cathedral or commercial glass) is available in many colors and degrees of transparency. It is even in thickness, though it is often textured. Hammered glass is a cathedral glass that has one side textured with uniform indentations that seem made with a small hammer. When the light hits the glass, the indentations act as facets that fracture the light. Opalescent glass is almost opaque. It is often used for making lampshades and other hand-crafted objects that will be viewed largely or entirely by reflected light (such as the necklaces on page 2227). Moss-backed and granite-backed glass have one rough side; the texture disperses the light passing through.

Today, artificial light often makes stained glass appear less brilliant than when natural light is the source of illumination. But electricity also creates new uses for stained glass—in lampshades, panels, and other artifacts that can be illuminated so they are more beautiful by night than by day.

The techniques used to hold pieces of glass together have also changed. Each joining method has its own possibilities and limitations which influence the design of the work. Leaded glass, using the lead-strip technique devised in the Middle Ages, is still in use (page 2229). To this has been added the copper-foil method (page 2226). Copper-foil work resembles leaded glass in that the foil outlines the glass pieces and becomes part of the design. But the thin, delicate foil works better than the heavier H-shaped lengths of lead in intricate, flowing designs, such as those of the Art Nouveau style. Tiffany lampshades were made this way. Three other techniques described here—glass lamination (page 2222), slab-glass casting (page 2223), and glass-mosaic assembly (page 2225)—are suggested for beginners, since the projects can be completed without cutting glass into precise shapes.

All these ways of working with glass can be used at home. A worktable by a window is an adequate studio if you do not attempt large projects. Care must be exercised in handling and cutting glass, of course. If you are a novice, wear goggles to protect your eyes, especially when you are tapping on the glass to deepen a score mark (page 2220). Use a bench brush to sweep up glass fragments—don't use your fingers. Few glass workers wear gloves, which are awkward because they slip, but if you don't, remember at all times that the glass edges can be razor sharp and can repay carelessness with a nasty gash.

The Glass

Luckily, the medieval legend that stained glass was made of melted rubies and emeralds is not true. Actually, stained glass work is relatively inexpensive. The glass is colored principally by the addition of metal oxides while it is in a molten state. Sometimes an artist will apply a pigment to the surface of the glass, then fuse it in a kiln. It is believed that one yellow colorant, silver nitrate, used this way gave rise to the term "stained glass." Stained glass is made in two ways. It can be hand blown, as it was in the Middle Ages (below), or it can be made by machine. Examples of hand-blown and machine-made stained glass are pictured opposite.

Hand-blown, or antique, glass is made today much as it was in medieval times. The glassblower dips his blowpipe into a pot of molten glass, then forms a bubble by blowing into the pipe.

In the United States, the glassblower then lowers the bubble into a cylindrical mold. The glass is blown some more until it takes on the shape of the mold, and is then removed from the mold.

This cylinder of stained glass will have its ends cut off and be cut lengthwise. A workman will then feed the cylinder into a flattening furnace where it settles into a sheet.

Stained glass comes in large sheets, so it must be cut to the size and shape you need for your project. Even if you buy the scrap glass that is recommended for beginners, the pieces will often be too large or the wrong shape. Glass cutting consists of two basic steps—scoring and snapping.

Tools and materials
Cutting glass requires special equipment. Shown above (top, left to right) are a jar containing absorbent cotton moistened with kerosene, glass cutter with ball end, combination snapping and grozing pliers (optional), grozing pliers, and breaking or snapping pliers. At the bottom right is clear window glass to be used for practicing; at the left is a scrap of stained glass. For a cutting surface, you can use insulation board, newspapers, magazines, or a scrap of carpeting. A resilient surface is needed because many types of glass have irregular surfaces, and because a yielding surface preserves the sharpness of the glass cutter. Have a table brush handy to clear your work surface of glass chips, and wear safety goggles to protect your eyes from flying glass splinters.

Scoring and snapping
Cutting glass requires that you first score the surface with a continuous, even scratch exactly where you want the glass to break. This is done with a glass cutter, a small steel wheel set into a metal or plastic shaft. To keep control of the glass cutter, always work standing up. Place the glass on the soft work surface and dip the wheel of the glass cutter into the kerosene-soaked cotton. (Do this before each cut to lubricate the wheel.)

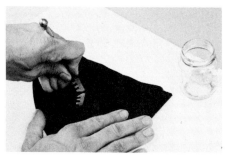

There are two ways to hold the cutter. The usual way is between the first two fingers and the thumb (above).

If you find the first grip awkward, try the second (above). Grasp the shaft with all four fingers and place your thumb at the top end. With either grip, keep the cutter perpendicular to the glass.

Beginning at the far edge of the glass, draw the cutter toward you in a single continuous motion from one edge to the other. Never stop, then start again in the middle of a score, and never go over a score twice. The most important aspect of scoring is the amount of pressure required by that particular type of glass. Only experience can teach you this. As a general rule, cut on the smoother side of textured glass. You can move the cutter quite rapidly, if you like, but you can also move it slowly as long as you make one continuous motion with consistent pressure.

The glass must be snapped immediately after a score is made (above). If you delay, the break is likely to be ragged or difficult, because of the tendency of glass to heal it-

self. To snap the glass, place a thumb on each side of the scored line and make a fist with each hand. Be careful not to touch the edge of the glass, which is likely to be dangerously sharp.

Exert leverage by twisting the wrists so the thumbs are pulled apart. The glass should snap cleanly in two (above). (Half the art of cutting glass lies in self-confidence, which comes rapidly with practice.)

Clean the new glass edges, removing the tiny, razor-sharp slivers, by scraping one against the other (above).

Aids in cutting
With some types of glass and with certain cuts, such as a curve, it is necessary to tap the glass to help fracture the score line. To do this, use the ball end of the glass cutter. With the scored side up, lift an edge of the glass and tap along the underside of the scored line until the score becomes a visual fracture. (If you are a beginner, wear safety goggles during this operation.) Then snap the glass with your hands as usual.

CUTTING GLASS

Occasionally you will want to cut a piece of glass that is too small to snap with your hands. In that case use breaking pliers to grip the edge of the glass, placing the front edge of the pliers' jaws against the scored line. Then exert leverage and snap (above).

If a snapped edge of glass is irregular, you can grind away the bumps with a grozing pliers (above). To work with this pliers, use the side of the jaws with a twisting motion.

If you have a combination snapping and grozing pliers, use the tip of the jaws to snip away irregularities along the edge of the glass (above).

Cutting with a pattern

Cutting glass into free shapes is relatively easy and several of the projects described here call for the use of small, randomly shaped pieces of scrap glass. However, if you wish to follow a design exactly, you will need to cut the glass into specific shapes, and you will need a pattern for each shape.

To cut glass precisely, place the pattern on top of the glass. Begin each score at the far edge of the glass and move the wheel of the cutter along the pattern edge (above). But when you reach a pattern corner, don't stop or try to turn; continue the score toward yourself until you have run the cutter off the edge of the glass nearest you. Break the score immediately. Then score along another side of the pattern, running the cutter off the edge each time and snapping each score immediately after it is made. This may seem wasteful, but it is the best way to cut, and so it saves glass in the long run. You can economize by placing each pattern piece so there is not more than ½ inch of waste to one side of the line that will be scored. Then use a breaking pliers to snap off the narrow strip of glass. If you try to place the pattern closer to the edge than this, you will find it difficult, if not impossible, to grip and break off the waste.

Most beginners tend to cut outside the pattern line, making their cut piece of glass too large. To avoid this, place the pattern edge about 1/64 inch short of the exact position for each successive score.

After snapping a score, especially a curved one, you will sometimes be left with an ear of glass where it did not break along the scored line. Snap off this irregularity with the breaking pliers (above). Remove smaller bumps with the grozing pliers.

Stained-glass suppliers

Supplies used for stained-glass projects may be ordered by mail from these companies. (Write for a catalogue first.)

Glass Masters Guild
621 Avenue of the Americas
New York, N.Y. 10011

Nervo Distributors
650 University Ave.
Berkeley, Calif. 94710

S.A. Bendheim Co., Inc.
122 Hudson St.
New York, N.Y. 10013

Whittemore-Durgin
803 Washington Ave.
Hanover, Mass. 02339

Suggested reading

Books

Adventures in Light and Color, by Charles J. Connick, Random House, New York, N.Y.

Glass Craft, by Kay Kinney, Chilton Book Co., Philadelphia, Pa.

Stained Glass, An Architectural Art, by Robert W. Sowers, Universe Books, New York, N.Y.

Stained Glass Crafting, by Paul W. Wood, Sterling Publications Co., Inc., New York, N.Y.

Stained Glass Primer, by Peter Mollica, Mollica Stained Glass Press, Berkeley, Calif.

Step-by-Step Stained Glass, by Erik Erikson, Western Publishing Co., Inc., Racine, Wisc.

The Lost Art, A Survey of 1000 Years of Stained Glass, by Robert Sowers, George Wittenborn, Inc., New York, N.Y.

The Technique of Stained Glass, by Patrick Reyntiens, Watson-Guptill Publications, New York, N.Y.

Working With Stained Glass, by Jean-Jacques Duval, Thomas Y. Crowell Co., New York, N.Y.

Periodicals

Glass Art Magazine, published bimonthly, P.O. Box 7527, Oakland, Calif. 94601

Stained Glass, published bimonthly. The Stained Glass Association of America, 1125 Wilmington Avenue, St. Louis, Mo. 63111.

The laminated glass sandwich, pictured in color at right, consists of four layers, with two outer sheets of clear glass and a filling of stained-glass scraps. They are held together with clear epoxy.

Using a technique called lamination, this panel is made by sandwiching two layers of stained glass fragments between two sheets of clear glass. Color laps color in a random design, creating an interesting mix in which some new colors are created.

Glass and Plastics

Laminated panel

The glass-lamination process uses a clear liquid epoxy to bond layers of stained glass fragments onto a solid base of clear glass. Panels made this way are pictured above and on page 2217. You can superimpose colors with this technique, depending on how many layers of colored glass you put in your sandwich. Since scraps of stained glass can be used, you do not need to master accurate glass cutting unless you want to follow a specific design. The method used to bond the glass layers is essentially the familiar one of gluing.

Materials
To make the panel shown above, you need two identical pieces of clear window glass (8 inches square is a manageable size). You also need: small scraps of stained glass (or scraps cut from larger pieces—see Craftnotes, pages 2220 and 2221); clear epoxy resin (the bonding agent); a stirring stick; and a shallow, disposable container such as a plastic jar lid in which to mix the two epoxy components. Epoxy that takes only five minutes to harden is available. To finish the edges of the panel, you need colored plastic tape or a metal section frame (sold in art supply stores).

Making the Panel
To make a panel with randomly shaped pieces of stained glass, first place a clear piece of glass on a light-colored surface. If you have access to the kind of horizontal light box that artists and photographers use—a box topped with frosted glass that has fluorescent or incandescent lights inside—use it to help you compose your arrangement. Put pieces of stained glass on the clear-glass base, arranging and rearranging them until the composition pleases you. Then, one by one, brush epoxy on the bottom of each piece, and press it into place on the base.

To prepare the epoxy for use, you need to mix the resin with the catalyst, following the manufacturer's directions. You may like the texture that results if bubbles are trapped when a piece of stained glass is laid down. If not, buy epoxy with a sufficiently long working time so you can let it set a bit after application, before laying the piece in place. Stir the epoxy slowly so you don't introduce bubbles, and slide the stained glass around, after you put it in position, to squeeze out bubbles.

For overlapping colors, arrange a second layer of stained glass pieces on top of the first. When you like the design, epoxy them to the first layer. Then put epoxy on top of the second layer of stained glass and lay the second square of clear glass over it, making sure all outer edges of the sandwich are lined up.

The glass panel pictured on page 2217 was made similarly, but in this case enough epoxy was mixed so it could be poured over each layer, completely embedding the glass fragments in the middle of the sandwich. When this type of lamination is used, the top piece of clear glass is optional, since the epoxy will keep the glass fragments dust free and provide a relatively smooth surface for cleaning.

Finishing
To give the panel a finished appearance, encase the edges with several layers of plastic tape. An alternative is to assemble a sectional metal picture frame and place the panel in it. The panel can be used as a trivet or a wall decoration, but it is most dramatically displayed by being hung in a window.

Using Patterns
If you do not like the random approach to design, you can, of course, plan your design in advance, and cut the glass to predetermined shapes. The best way to make such a design is to use colored sheets of transparent, adhesive-backed plastic, corresponding to the colors of the glass you plan to use. (Such plastic is available in art-supply stores.) Plan each layer with pieces of colored plastic; then make a paper pattern of each shape, marking the color on it. Use these patterns when you cut the glass (Craftnotes, page 2221). Place the first layer of the design beneath the clear-glass base to serve as a guide while you epoxy the pieces of glass you have cut to the base. Repeat with each successive layer.

Windows and Frames
You can use an existing window as the base for a laminated panel. Leaving the window glass in its sash, remove the window from its frame, and lay it horizontally on a level surface. Arrange and epoxy the stained glass in place. Then use a second sheet of clear window glass, cut to fit into the sash, as the top layer. Apply epoxy around the edges of the top layer to make the sandwich airtight and dustproof.

Yet another alternative is to start with a box-type picture frame of clear plastic. Do the laminating of stained glass inside the plastic box.

Glass and Plastics
Slab-glass casting $ ◨ 👫 🔥

Slab glass is very thick—generally ¾ inch. It usually comes in 8-by-12-inch pieces. Cutting such slab glass at home is very difficult, but you can buy scrap chunks and set them in plaster panels to mount in a frame for a window, a screen, or a room divider. They can also be installed in a wall. The plaster, poured between the chunks of heavy glass, holds them together without blocking the passage of light through the glass.

Materials
When you buy scrap pieces of slab glass, make sure they are full thickness, not thin or irregular shards. To make the 12-inch square panel shown at right, you need about two dozen pieces of glass. You also need: a plywood board at least 16 inches square (the base you will work on); ¾-by-¾-inch strips of wood, two 12 inches long and two 14 inches long (to make the frame that will contain the wet plaster); masking tape; a sheet of clear adhesive-backed plastic at least 16 inches square; nails; hammer; plaster of paris; and a container and stick for mixing the plaster.

Designing the Panel
Take advantage of the rugged nature of the slab glass when you design your panel. You can try a figurative design if you like, but a bold, simple, geometric design is more appropriate and easier to handle. If you want to plan your design in advance,

Chunks of ¾-inch-thick slab glass, also known as *dalle de verre*, form a bold, jewel like pattern in this panel in which they are cast in plaster.

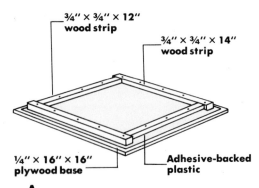

¾" × ¾" × 12"
wood strip

¾" × ¾" × 14"
wood strip

¼" × 16" × 16"
plywood base

Adhesive-backed
plastic

A
Figure A: To make a frame to hold the plaster for a slab-glass panel, nail strips of wood to a plywood base which has been covered with adhesive-backed plastic, adhesive side up. Position the strips, then nail down the shorter strips first.

For easy handling, start with panels no larger than 12 inches square. You can install several small adjoining panels in a frame or wall, as shown here, if you want one large panel.

use pieces of colored paper cut to match your pieces of glass. Arrange them on a 12-inch square of black paper. (When light shines through your finished panel, the plaster that holds the glass together will appear black.) Mark a 1-inch border around the edge of the black paper; to maintain structural strength in the actual panel, do not let any of the colored pieces project into this border as you arrange them, and keep the pieces at least ¼ inch apart. When you are satisfied with the composition, paste the pieces down.

Making the Panel
To start the mold in which you will cast the panel, cover the plywood base with the clear plastic, adhesive side up. (If you have prepared a design, tape it to the board under the plastic.) Nail the strips of wood to the plywood to form a frame that will hold the liquid plaster (Figure A). Cover the inside edge of each strip of wood with masking tape. Carefully position each piece of slab glass on the adhesive plastic, following your pattern or making a random design. The adhesive on the plastic will keep the pieces of glass from shifting when you pour the liquid plaster of paris around them and it will keep plaster from seeping under the glass where it would block the light.

Make sure the mold is level. Mix the plaster of paris with water, following the package directions. Approximately one part plaster to one part water should give you the right consistency—thin enough so it will level itself but not so runny that it will not harden properly. You need about four cups of liquid plaster to make a 12-inch square panel. Pour the plaster slowly between the chunks of glass and around the edge, trying to avoid getting plaster on the top surface of the glass pieces. Stop pouring when the plaster is level with the glass.

When it has set, scrape off any plaster that may have been spilled on the glass. But leave the frame in place until the plaster is completely set—up to one hour. Remove the frame, being careful not to chip the plaster edges.

Other Possibilities
If you do not like the look of the plain white plaster, you can sprinkle a thin layer of sand around the glass pieces before you pour the plaster, and add a thin layer of sand to the top of the plaster while it is still soft. When the plaster is hard, brush away excess sand. Alternatively, you can color the plaster with tempera powder or food coloring as you mix it.

Or, instead of plaster, consider using an opaque epoxy. Plaster is cheaper and easier to work with, but epoxy is stronger, more durable, lighter, and waterproof. Following the directions that come with the epoxy, mix the two components; then proceed as though you were using plaster. Epoxy is thicker than plaster, so a small piece of cardboard is useful in coaxing it tight against the edges of the glass.

Interesting mosaics can be made with random pieces of stained-glass remnants, arranged in a haphazard design, as was done here. You could duplicate this design by tracing the shapes in this full-sized photograph to make patterns for cutting glass in these shapes.

Glass and Plastics
Glass mosaic

To make a mosaic with stained glass, you bond a single layer of pieces of the colored glass to a base layer of clear glass. Mirrored glass can also be used as a base, if the colors of the stained glass are light enough to let the mirrored surface show through. Then you work an opaque grout into the spaces between the colored pieces. In contrast to most stained-glass work, the irregularity of the dark line that separates the colors is characteristic of this technique. If you like you can use the design shown above; cut pieces of stained glass to match this pattern. This is a good place to practice glass cutting; imperfect cuts will be hardly noticeable because the spaces between the pieces are so irregular. If you prefer, develop your own design, arranging random scraps of glass.

Materials
To duplicate the 4¾-by-8¼-inch panel shown, you will need: the glass-cutting tools listed on page 2220, scraps of stained glass in whatever colors you like; a 4¾-by-8¼-inch piece of clear glass for the base; paper for patterns; ruler; pencil; felt-tipped pens or colored pencils; grease pencil; clear epoxy to bind the stained glass to the base; a wooden tongue depressor or strip of cardboard for spreading the epoxy; grout (opaque epoxy that you can color, or liquid solder that comes in a tube); container and stirrer to mix the epoxy; ¾-by-¾-inch strips of wood, two 4¾ inches long and two at least 10 inches long, for the frame; hammer; nails; and a piece of plywood at least 10 inches square to use as a work surface.

Erik Erikson's light-catching rainbowlike mobile illustrates the adaptability of the copper-foil joining technique, also used to make the necklaces shown opposite.

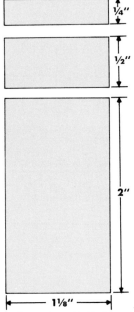

B

Figure B: To make patterns for the blue stained-glass pendant pictured (opposite, top center), follow these measurements. Mark the outlines on heavy paper with pencil and ruler. Then cut out the patterns and use them to cut the glass pieces.

Making and Using a Pattern

Trace the design on page 2225. Color the shapes that will be glass with felt-tipped markers or colored pencils. Cut the pattern pieces apart; then use a grease pencil to trace the outline of each piece onto glass of the appropriate color. Following the directions in the Craftnotes on page 2221, cut out each glass shape. Do not try to correct any edges that do not exactly conform to the pattern.

Cementing and Grouting

Cementing the stained-glass pieces to the clear-glass base is the most important step. Positioning determines the spaces between the pieces. And careful application of epoxy keeps the opaque grout from seeping under the colored glass.

Tape the colored-paper pattern pieces in position on the plywood work surface. Put the clear-glass base over this pattern, and frame it by nailing the ¾-by-¾-inch strips of wood to the plywood (Figure A, page 2224). This frame will hold the base glass and grout in place as you work. Put strips of masking tape on the inside faces of the wood so the epoxy will not bond it to the glass.

Mix the clear epoxy, following the package directions, and spread a thick coat of it on the clear glass with a tongue depressor or cardboard strip. This is the best way to keep grout from seeping under the colored glass. Place the cut pieces of glass in the layer of epoxy, following the pattern underneath. (As an alternative, you can butter the underside of each colored piece with epoxy; then place it on the base glass.) To further prevent grout seepage, pour a little additional clear epoxy in the spaces between the pieces. Following the directions on the package, wait for the clear epoxy to harden before applying the opaque grout.

If you like the effect, you can add a black colorant when you mix opaque epoxy resin and catalyst. This was done in the project pictured on page 2225. Carefully pour the grout into the spaces between the colored pieces. Make the grout thin enough so it will pour easily. Do your best to keep the grout off the surface of the glass; removing it is both difficult and messy. If you do happen to drop some where you don't want it, you will have to remove it immediately with a damp cloth or later with acetone.

For added texture, you can sprinkle sand onto the grout when it begins to set. Or, instead of using opaque epoxy, you can substitute liquid solder. This dries to resemble lead, and it can be applied as it comes, straight from the tube.

When the grout has hardened, remove the wood strips. The panel is now ready for framing and hanging in front of an existing window, or to be set into a room divider or a coffee-table top.

Glass and Plastics
Copper-foiled necklace

The use of adhesive-backed copper foil as a means of joining pieces of stained glass lends itself to the delicate task of making stained-glass costume jewelry. The directions that follow are for making the blue necklace of opalescent glass pictured opposite, top center. Similar techniques were used to create the variations pictured opposite, top left and right, including one made of fragments of red slab glass.

Materials

In addition to the glass-cutting tools listed in the Craftnotes (page 2220), you will need: a soldering gun or iron (the pencil-tip iron is best for delicate work); a spool of solder; flux (oleic acid or zinc chloride) and a small brush to apply it; ¼- or 3/16-inch-wide adhesive-backed copper foil; a smooth, flat stick to burnish the foil onto the glass; 14- or 16-gauge copper wire (for loops and links); 10- or 12-gauge copper wire (for the neck ring); steel wool; needle-nosed pliers; detergent; copper-sulfate solution; paste wax or clear nail polish; and liver of sulfate.

Cutting and Wrapping the Glass

Make a pattern of heavy paper for each glass shape. Follow the measurements in Figure B, or use a design of your own. Referring to the Craftnotes (pages 2220 and 2221), cut out the pieces of stained glass. Then, wrap the edges of each piece with adhesive-backed copper foil (photographs 1 through 5, page 2228).

You can wear stained glass in the form of costume jewelry. Erik Erikson, who usually designs large stained-glass windows, combined copper foil, copper wire, and solder with fragments of stained glass to make these necklaces. The baroque bauble (left) was made with bits of red slab glass. Opalescent rectangles of stained glass (center and right) were strung together with links of copper wire.

CRAFTNOTES: SOLDERING

Soldering is a means of joining two pieces of metal using a third metal, called solder. The solder, an alloy of tin and lead, comes in the form of wire wound on a spool. It melts at a lower temperature than the metals being joined, so it flows between them, forming a bridge as it hardens. The solder used most often for stained glass work is 60/40 solder (60 percent tin and 40 percent lead).

In stained-glass work, edges of the pieces of colored glass are encased in lead came (a tin-and-lead alloy) or copper foil. Joining these metals does not require much heat, so a solder that melts at low temperature can be used. A heated soldering iron is used to melt the solder onto the metal-encased edges of the glass, without melting that metal or heating the glass. When the solder cools, the pieces are joined. Use a soldering iron with care; the hot tip can give you a painful burn. Always rest the heated iron on its holder between uses, and keep it away from such flammable materials as paper patterns that it might ignite.

It is necessary to clean the metal so the solder will adhere properly. Lead came is cleaned by abrasion of the metal with steel wool (above).

This is followed by cleaning the surface chemically, using a mild acid called flux that removes the oxide that accumulates on the surface with exposure to air (above). Flux is applied with a brush. Copper foil usually needs only to be brushed with flux (oleic acid or zinc chloride) to be cleaned. Be careful not to get flux on skin or clothing.

Using the soldering iron
Before you begin to solder, prepare the tip of the iron by tinning it. Heat the iron, brush a bit of oleic acid or soldering paste on the tip; then touch the end of the solder wire to the iron tip, depositing a thin coat of solder. This is called tinning.

To solder, hold the heated soldering iron in one hand and the spool of solder wire in the other. Place the end of the solder on the joint of the lead came or copper foil. Hold the soldering-iron tip next to the solder; it will melt and flow into the joint to hold the pieces together (above).

Keeping the tip clean
Keep a wet cellulose sponge handy to periodically wipe off the discoloration and residue that gather on the hot tip. Simply rub the hot tip quickly across the wet sponge.

1: Thin copper foil is used to edge stained-glass pieces for joining. It comes in a roll with a backing that is peeled off so the adhesive is exposed.

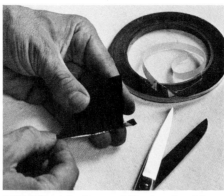

2: Stick the strip of copper foil to the edge of the piece of stained glass. Make sure the glass edge is centered on the foil.

3: When the entire piece of glass is encircled with foil, cut the foil, leaving approximately ¼ inch overlap.

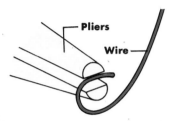

C
Figure C: To form a loop at the end of a piece of copper wire, grasp it between the jaws of a needle-nosed pliers. Twist until you have formed a ¼-inch-long closed loop in the wire.

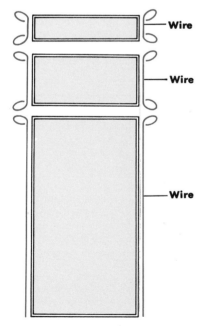

D
Figure D: Solder lengths of wire with looped ends to the foil-wrapped sides of the glass pieces. Small and medium pieces need wires looped at both ends. The large end piece needs a wire looped at the top only. Before you solder, make sure the loops are closed so they do not unlink later.

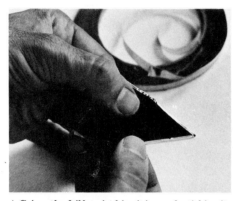

4: Crimp the foil by pinching it inward, sticking it to the glass, and encasing the edge.

5: After crimping, use a smooth, flat stick to burnish and flatten the crimped edges of the foil.

Soldering

Using a small paintbrush, apply flux to the foil on each piece. Referring to the Craftnotes on page 2227, apply a very thin layer of solder on all the foiled edges. Do not let the heated iron rest too long on the foil, or the adhesive will melt.

Rub the copper wire with steel wool; then cut four 1¼-inch lengths of the wire, four 1½-inch lengths, and two 2½-inch pieces. Using needle-nosed pliers, form a ¼-inch loop at one end of the 2½-inch lengths and at both ends of the shorter lengths of wire (Figure C).

One at a time, solder the wire to the foil-edged glass (Figure D). Brush flux on each wire and heat the soldering iron. Place the wire against the solder-coated foiled edge of the glass piece, and then press the heated soldering iron against the wire. The solder on the foil will melt and attach the wire. Apply a small amount of additional solder to strengthen the bond.

Now apply a heavier, rounded layer of solder over both wire and foil. This is called beading and gives dimension and support to the foil so it is less likely to come off. Finally, put a thin layer of solder on the loops to give the pieces a unified color. After each wire is soldered in place, wash off all flux residue with detergent.

To impart a coppery finish, put copper-sulfate solution on all soldered areas. Use a soft cloth and rub vigorously. Then polish the coppered solder with paste wax or coat it with clear nail polish to preserve the coppery finish and make it shine.

Linking

Join the separate pieces with links of copper wire. Assemble them in descending order of size, as pictured on page 2227. To make the links, use the needle-nosed pliers to form ten small coils from the same gauge of wire soldered onto the glass. To form the coil, hold the end of the wire in the jaws of the pliers, and wind the wire around one jaw twice. Pull the coils apart slightly—just enough to pass the link through two adjoining loops (Figure E). Then squeeze the coils together with the pliers to make the joining secure.

Finishing

When all the glass pieces have been linked, make a neck ring from the heavier wire. Cut off a piece of wire (the length will vary with the wearer; the one pictured measures 24 inches). Curve the wire by grasping both ends with pliers and working it back and forth against a hard, round post or table leg. With the needle-nosed pliers, make an open loop or hook in each end of the neck ring. Attach the pendant to the ring with the remaining links. Apply a darkening solution of liver of sulfate on the neck ring and coils. Protect the newly antiqued copper parts with a coat of wax or clear nail polish. To wear the necklace, hook the neck-ring loops together in back.

Glass and Plastics
Leaded stained-glass panel $ ● ⅄ ⚚

The traditional technique of joining pieces of stained glass with strips of lead was used to make this panel. The simple design employs only straight glass cuts, making it a good introduction for a novice. The lead technique has changed little since it was devised in the Middle Ages, when magnificent cathedral windows were made of stained glass.

H-shaped strips of lead, called came, have been used for centuries as a means of joining pieces of stained glass for architectural installations. Lead came is durable, easily cut and soldered, and weatherproof. Hence it is appropriate for large stained-glass windows. The procedure used in making a leaded window is not complex, but it demands exacting craftsmanship because the glass pieces and lead strips between them must be fitted together with precision. If one piece is slightly inaccurate, it can throw everything else out of position. The panel shown above is small enough to be a good introduction to this technique.

Materials

To make a 6-inch-square leaded-glass panel, you need: the glass-cutting tools listed in the Craftnotes on page 2220; carbon paper; one 6-foot strip of ¼-inch flat H-shaped lead came; 60/40 solder; oleic acid (flux); soldering iron and stand; steel wool; lightweight paper for diagrams and heavier paper for patterns; pencil; ruler; scissors; pattern shears; ½-inch plywood at least 10 inches square; masking tape; four ¾-inch strips of wood at least 6 inches long; a lead stretcher; hammer; glazing nails; lead knife; needle-nosed pliers; small block of wood; and copper wire.

Completed link

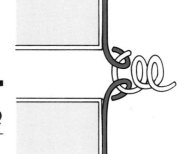

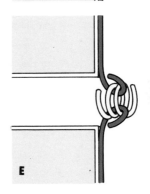

E

Figure E: To join the pieces of glass, use needle-nosed pliers to form spiral links (top). Then insert the coil in the two loops to be joined (center right), turning it until both loops are joined (bottom, right). Compress the coil with pliers to flatten it.

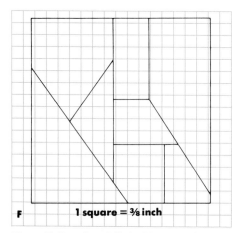

F   1 square = ⅜ inch

Figure F: To make a full-sized drawing of the design for the leaded glass panel, enlarge the design above by copying it, square by square, onto paper you have ruled in ⅜-inch squares.

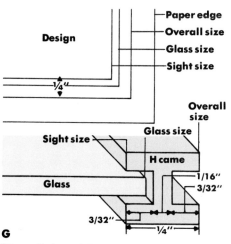

G

Figure G: Around the border of your pattern, called a cartoon, draw parallel lines that correspond to the dimensions of the strips of H-shaped lead came used to frame the panel (top). The sight-size line indicates glass that will remain visible. The glass-size line indicates the actual outer edge of the glass that will be hidden by the lead strips. The overall-size line indicates the outer edge of the lead came (detail, lower right). Standard measurements for ¼-inch lead came are shown, but double-check them against your strips.

6: An invaluable aid in cutting accurate patterns for stained-glass work is pattern shears. Its triple blades remove a sliver of paper equal to the space needed by the heart of the H-shaped lead came that is placed between the glass pieces to hold them together.

Cutting the Glass

Enlarge the design for the panel (Figure F), or use a design of your own. To make your own, start with a 6-inch square. Divide it with a few straight lines. For your first project, limit the number of pieces to about ten. Work with straight lines, since they are easier to cut than curves.

The full-sized drawing of the design is called a cartoon; the next step is to indicate on this cartoon the thickness of the lead came that will frame the panel. The outer line on the cartoon (Figure F) indicates the glass size; it does not take into account the thickness of the lead came. Referring to Figure G, draw an additional line around the cartoon to indicate the overall size. If you are working with a design of your own, draw the sight size also—the glass that will not be hidden by lead strips—to make sure that no crucial part of the design will be covered.

Use the cartoon to make two copies of the design, an assembly diagram and a pattern diagram. Make a sandwich with the cartoon on top, then carbon paper, lightweight assembly diagram paper, carbon paper, and heavy pattern paper. Tack or tape the paper sandwich down so the sheets will not shift. With a pencil, go over all of the lines of the design, including the sight size, glass size, and overall size. To keep track of the pieces, number each that will be cut from glass. The pattern diagram will be cut into individual patterns for cutting the glass; so it is transferred onto heavy paper at the bottom of the sandwich. The assembly diagram will be used as a guide when you assemble the glass pieces. Save the cartoon for future reference in case you want to duplicate the design.

The next step is to cut the pattern diagram into individual pieces. First, use regular scissors to cut along the glass-size lines. Then use the pattern shears to cut apart the design, forming an individual pattern for each glass piece (photograph 6). Pattern shears are special triple-bladed scissors that cut away a thin strip of the pattern that is equal to the thickness of the heart of the lead came. When they are used, the glass pieces and lead can be assembled without increasing the overall size of the panel.

Following the directions in the Craftnotes (pages 2220 and 2221), cut a piece of stained glass to match each pattern piece. When all the pieces have been cut, you are ready to assemble them.

Assembling the Panel

Lead came must be stretched and straightened to remove the kinks before it can be used. You can use a lead stretcher (photograph 7); or you can enlist the aid of a friend with a second pair of pliers; or you can step on one end of the lead came and pull on it, stretching it up parallel with your body. Whether you use stretcher, friend, or foot, untwist the lead as you stretch it. Handle the stretched lead carefully; it can be stretched only once.

Tape the assembly diagram on the plywood work surface. Then, in the lower left-hand corner, nail two strips of wood at a right angle along the overall-size lines of the diagram. (Check the angle with a right triangle.) Cut two lengths of came slightly longer than the sides of the design. To cut the lead, use a sharp lead knife and gentle rolling pressure (photograph 8). If cutting causes the lead channels to collapse, pry them open again with needle-nosed pliers. Place the came along the wood strips to form the bottom and left sides of the panel. Tap in a nail at each end to keep the lead in place (photograph 9).

Insert the first piece of glass in the lower left-hand corner (photograph 9). Make certain that it corresponds to its outline on the assembly diagram. To make sure the glass is seated in its channels, place a small block of wood against the edge and tap the block gently with a hammer. Do this to every piece you insert.

Next, lay a piece of stretched came along the exposed edge of the glass. Mark the angle where it meets the other lead strips (photograph 10), and cut it. Continue assembling the glass, piece by piece, cutting lengths of lead came to fit and gradually fanning out from the starting corner. After adding each piece, lightly hammer in glazing nails to hold the glass snugly in place as you measure, mark, and cut the came (photograph 11). Then remove the nails as you fit the next piece.

If you have difficulty matching the glass pieces with the lines of the assembly diagram, check the glass against the patterns. Nibble an edge down with grozing pliers if necessary to obtain a good fit.

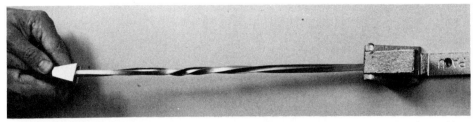

7: To straighten the crinkled lead came for use, clamp one one in a lead stretcher. Grip the other end in the jaws of any type of pliers, and pull until you feel the lead stretch and see it straighten.

8: To cut a strip of lead came to length, place it on the wood work surface and rock the lead-cutting knife blade gently as you press it down.

9: Insert the first piece of stained glass in the corner of the lead strips, sliding its edges into the open channels of the lead.

10: To mark the soft lead came for cutting, score it with a fingernail wherever it meets another strip at an angle. Then cut it with the lead knife.

11: To keep the pieces of glass from shifting as you work, secure each additional strip of lead came with temporary nails. This will insure a snug fit.

When all the pieces are in place, finish the top and right sides with strips of lead came cut to the overall size, and trim away the excess at the bottom and left side. Nail two more strips of wood beside the two final cames to hold everything in place as you solder.

Soldering

Referring to the Craftnotes (page 2227), apply solder to the individual pieces of came where they butt each other. Rub each of these joints with a piece of steel wool to clean the surface; then apply flux to the area with a brush. In general, use as little solder as possible. While soldering, be careful not to melt the lead came itself. Some soldering irons heat rapidly, and a fraction of a second can make a great deal of difference. Repairing melted lead came is difficult and time-consuming. It can be avoided. Have a scrap of came on hand for testing the heated iron; if the iron melts the came, turn it off. When it has cooled to the point where it will not melt the came while it is resting on it, it will still melt solder.

When all the joints on the front of the panel have been soldered, remove the strips of wood, turn the panel over and solder the joints on the back.

If you wish to hang the panel in front of a window, solder on two loops of copper wire. Clean the wire with steel wool, and form small loops by bending the wire with needle-nosed pliers. Cover the loops with a thin coat of solder; then attach one to each top corner of the panel.

For related entries, see "Acrylics," "Casting," "Glass Working," "Greeting Cards," "Jewelry," "Leaded Glass," "Molding Methods," and "Mosaics."

STAMP DECOUPAGE

Philatelic Patchwork

Ruth Wilson Newkirk, a native of Massachusetts, lives in New York. Among Ruth's many interests is stamp collecting. When her friends heard about this hobby, they began sending her stamps. Soon she had so many duplicates that she began using them as a craft material. Her stamp collages are displayed at Adventures in Crafts in New York.

The penny magenta from British Guiana is a one-cent stamp that was issued in a limited edition in 1856. This stamp is No. 13 of a series found by a British schoolboy more than 100 years ago. It was purchased by Irwin Weinberg, a Pennsylvania stamp dealer, in 1970 at a private auction for $280,000. Subsequently this stamp, slightly larger than an average postage stamp, rose in value to $325,000. Pictured in the center of the stamp is a sailing ship. In Latin, "We give and we seek in turn" is printed across the top and bottom edges. In script on the left side of the stamp are sets of postmasters' initials.

Postage stamps are noteworthy collectibles, but the ones most of us come across—stamps of no present value to philatelists—can be used as a bright and interesting craft material. Purchased by the pound or peeled from envelopes, common stamps can be used to cover tabletops, boxes, and wastepaper baskets to make colorful one-of-a-kind collages. The work is easy, the cost is low, and the results can be delightful. (Should you come across a stamp that strikes you as unusual, perhaps because of age or a printing flaw, by all means check it out with a collector. The most valuable stamp in the world—the penny magenta from British Guiana, pictured above—was found by a schoolboy. It is worth more than a quarter of a million dollars, more for its size and weight than any other substance in the world.)

To make stamp collages, any common contemporary stamps in good condition can be used. But unless you are seeking a special effect, discard stamps that are torn or heavily cancelled. Usually your goal will be to achieve a uniform tapestry effect, with no single stamp standing out from its neighbors, as shown in the close-up view of a stamp-covered wastebasket, opposite.

Scavenging for Stamps

The easiest and least expensive way to gather stamps for craftwork is to ask friends and relatives to save used stamps for you. A slower but more interesting way to get foreign stamps is to establish correspondence with people in other countries. Organizations such as Letters Abroad, 209 East 56th Street, New York, N.Y. 10022 provide teachers and recreation leaders with the names and addresses of teen-agers and adults seeking correspondence in all parts of the world. Consulates, too, can help you establish this type of correspondence.

If you are trying to locate domestic stamps of a particular type, start with an inquiry at your local post office. The postal service provides authoritative advice for stamp collectors. In the telephone book, you can locate stamp dealers and companies that package low-cost stamp kits for beginning collectors. Some variety

Stamps from all corners of the globe were glued to a wastebasket to make this philatelic patchwork, then were protected with several coats of decoupage varnish. Although rare, torn, or heavily cancelled stamps are not recommended for craftwork, it is not difficult to find thousands of suitable specimens.

stores and department stores sell stamps, and many magazines carry advertisements offering mail-order stamps. If you become so fascinated by stamps that you decide to switch from decorating with them to collecting them, daily newspapers often publish information about stamp clubs and exhibits.

Lift Off

To remove stamps from envelopes and ready them for craft work, you will need: scissors; a bowl or basin; paper towels; waxed paper; a weight such as a heavy book; an empty cardboard or plastic shoe box about 6 by 12 inches; several packages of envelopes that will fit in the box; and a pencil.

Cut the stamps from their envelopes with scissors, leaving ¼ inch of paper around each stamp. Then soak the stamps in lukewarm water. The number of stamps to be soaked determines what soaking container you use. A large project such as the wastebasket shown on page 2237 requires about 400 stamps; when I need this many, I soak about 100 stamps at a time in my bathroom lavatory. Fill the container with water and soak the stamps for about ten minutes or until the glue backing becomes gummy (photograph 1). Any stamps glued to colored paper should be soaked individually; the paper dye sometimes runs and discolors stamps.

Meanwhile, prepare a drying sleeve for the wet stamps by folding a sheet of waxed paper large enough so you can mark a 6-by-12-inch section to receive stamps and have enough extra paper to cover them without blocking air circulation (photograph 2). One at a time, lift the soaked stamps out of the water, and slide them off their backing. Place the stamps on the waxed paper, face up and at least ¼ inch apart. Waxed paper is a good drying surface because any patches of glue remaining on the backs of the stamps will not stick to it as the stamp dries. When the 6-inch-wide section in the middle of the waxed paper is covered with stamps, close the sleeve carefully and set it aside in a place where air circulates freely. When the stamps are dry, put a heavy book over the sleeve to press the stamps flat. In three or four days, the stamps will be ready for craft use.

Sorting Stamps

When your stamps are dry and flat, examine them with a magnifying glass. I find Christmas stamps especially beautiful. You can select your favorites from many collecting categories—commemoratives, wildlife, airmail, flowers, presidents and world leaders, humanitarians, health organizations, transportation, religion, aerospace, sports, flags, explorers, educators, peace, or the arts. The easiest way to sort stamps is to place those of one category together. This is adequate either for a hodgepodge design or for one requiring one category of stamps, such as the collage of animals opposite, below. You could also sort stamps by color, shape, or size. These characteristics become important when you plan a balanced design such as the tabletop shown on page 2237.

Put each category of stamps in a single envelope and write the topic on the inner flap. With the flap up and the label facing you, put the envelope in a shoe box (photograph 3). Then you can leaf through the envelopes easily to locate any particular stamp in a hurry.

1: Soak a batch of stamps in a bowl of lukewarm water for about ten minutes to loosen the glue so you can slide each stamp off its paper backing and onto a sheet of waxed paper, face up. For more than 100 stamps, use a larger soaking container.

2: Fold waxed paper over the wet stamps to form a drying sleeve which will keep the stamps in place but allow air to circulate; they will not stick to the waxed surface. When the stamps are dry, press them flat in their sleeve with a heavy book.

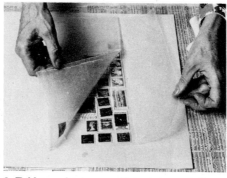

3: Sort the dry stamps according to topic into small envelopes, and write the category on the inner flap. Put the envelopes in a shoebox with the flaps up and the labels in alphabetical order. Then you can quickly find any stamp you are seeking.

Designs and Decorations
Pieced pictures

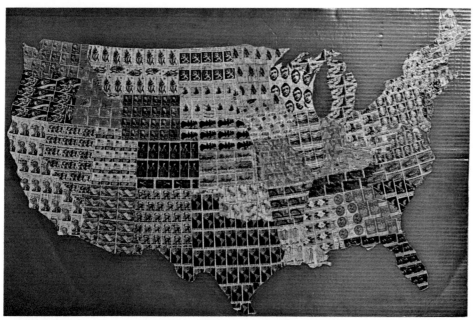

A map of the United States invites a stamp collage, the stamps being selected for their color, their pattern, or even for the affinity of the subject matter for a particular state.

Stamps pasted over small paper cutouts (page 2236) make these collages of ducks and giraffes. The cutouts were glued to construction paper, and backgrounds were added to make the pictures suitable for framing.

A

Figure A: As the starting point for a stamp collage, you can use a pencil and tracing paper to copy any of these patterns, or you can select interesting silhouettes elsewhere to trace. Transfer the pattern to bond paper with carbon paper; then use manicure scissors to cut it out.

4: To make a stamp collage in animal form, trace a design on bond paper and cut it out carefully; then glue stamps over the face of the cutout until all of the bond paper is covered.

5: Turn the decorated cutout over, and use manicure scissors to trim off the stamp edges, following the edges of the original cutout.

Any design can be cut out of paper and covered with stamps to make a collage silhouette, as was done with the United States map and the ducks and giraffes on page 2235. Several full-sized patterns are given in Figure A for you to trace, or you can find ideas in nature books, comic books, or on greeting cards. In addition to the pattern, you will need: tracing paper; scissors; a pencil; masking tape; white glue; stamps; colored paper; felt-tipped markers; and a picture frame if you decide to display the collage.

To begin, trace the design and cut it out. If an area of the design is narrow, as is the tail of a giraffe, reinforce the paper at that point on the face of the pattern using a small piece of masking tape. The size of the design will determine the number of stamps of one color and type that are needed; only a few are needed for one of the Figure A patterns, but in the map nearly two dozen went into Texas alone. Glue the stamps on the front of the cutout, beginning at one side of the cutout and letting the stamps overlap its edges (photograph 4). Set the covered cutout aside to dry. Then turn the cutout wrong side up so its outline is visible. With scissors, clip off stamp edges and masking tape, following the outline of the cutout (photograph 5). Glue the cutout, now a stamp collage, onto a sheet of construction paper. You can fill the background with other stamp collages or draw designs with felt-tipped markers, colored pens, or crayons. You can frame the collage, or use it as a greeting card. The same technique can be used to decorate a large map. To make the map collage on page 2235 I cut out each state along its boundary lines. Then I covered each cutout with stamps held in place with white glue. Once the glue was dry, I trimmed the stamp edges and assembled the map like a giant jigsaw puzzle, then glued the pieces onto a large sheet of colored mat board.

Designs and Decorations
Container decoupage

Special stamps showing favorite things—here, paintings, wildlife, love, skiing, stamp collecting, and sports—can be used to decorate a brightly colored box. By letting the background color show through, an informal balance is achieved between the colors and shapes of the stamps and the box.

A variety of stamps was glued at random over each panel of this wastebasket. Some stamps abut, others overlap. The inside of the container is lined with magazine pictures. Velvet ribbon and gold rickrack near the rim and the base provide added decoration.

A table that was stained with glass rings was restored to use by covering it with triangular and rectangular stamps, arranged in a symmetrical pattern that radiates out from the center. The stamps are protected with six coats of decoupage varnish.

Stamp collages lend themselves well to decoupage—the process of decorating surfaces with paper cutouts. Wood surfaces are the easiest to decorate, but any metal, stone, or plastic surface can be covered if it is properly prepared. A flat surface such as a tray or a tabletop (page 2237, bottom right) is a good place to start because you can lay out your design and see how each stamp will look before you begin gluing. Then you might try your hand at decorating old boxes, picture frames, or buckets. Items like these can be purchased at little cost at flea markets, tag sales, and thrift shops. The instructions here are for decorating the box and wastebasket pictured on page 2237, but they can be used for covering any flat surface. Decoupage materials are available at many craft stores, or by mail from Adventures in Crafts, Inc., 218 East 81st Street, New York, N.Y. 10028.

Materials needed in addition to stamps are: newspapers; fine sandpaper; clear acrylic spray fixative; white glue; an empty plastic container; sponge; rags; quick-drying clear varnish; a ½-inch-wide nylon brush; and turpentine. If you want to line a box or basket, you can use magazine photographs, gift wrap, wallpaper, acrylic paint, or even old postcards, menus, or greeting cards. For trimming, you need scissors and velvet ribbon, tassels, or braiding.

Arranging the Stamps

Stamps were applied to the box and the wastebasket shown on page 2237 in similar fashion. But on the box, I let the background color show through, making it a part of the design. On the wastebasket, stamps cover the entire outside surface. The edges of some stamps covering the wastebasket meet, while others overlap. I generally let the stamp's perforations show because I find their pattern contributes to the design and makes stamps more stamplike. Plan a design for the object you have chosen to decorate. You may want to make a bouquet with stamps picturing flowers. Or you may want to use stamps of the same size but of contrasting colors to make a balanced crisscross or banded design. Try to estimate the number of stamps you will need so you can have them ready. I used 400 stamps for the wastebasket.

Fastening Stamps

Cover your work surface with newspapers, and make sure the object to be decorated is clean. Smooth any rough spots or uneven edges with sandpaper or an emery board; then dust again. If you are covering a smooth, shiny surface of metal or plastic, you can make sure the glue holds by spraying the surfaces inside and out with acrylic fixative, or you can rub all surfaces with fine sandpaper until they have enough tooth to hold glue.

To speed gluing, you can pour several tablespoons of white glue into a plastic container such as an empty margarine tub. Dip the wrong side of a stamp in the glue. Use a scrap of cardboard to spread the glue evenly over the back of the stamp, including the perforated edges. Starting at the middle of the top edge of the container, glue the stamp in place. Use your fingers to straighten the stamp until it lies flat. Wipe off any excess glue with a damp sponge or a damp paper towel. Follow the lines of the container as you work from top to bottom (photograph 6) until your design is complete. You can wrap stamps over corner edges for a neat, smooth finish. I find I can cover about 100 square inches in an evening.

Liners

It is best to decorate the inside of the container before varnishing it. If you are using paint, apply it before you apply the stamps. But I often use magazine covers, menus, or greeting cards to line the inside. If you collect postcards, you can incorporate them in the design. Soak the cards, face up, in lukewarm water for ten minutes. Then use a butter knife to peel off the cardboard backing so you have a picture thin enough to glue. If you use larger pieces of paper such as gift wrap or wallpaper, cut separate pieces as necessary to conform to the interior wall. If you are working with a square wastebasket, for example, trace the shape of each exterior wall on the back of the paper. Add ¼ inch to each side edge of two panels that will face each other. Cut out each piece. Then glue the two pieces with seam allowances to opposite walls of the container. The extra width will overlap the corners to make a neat seam. Glue the remaining pieces in place. To remove air bubbles, press the lining with your hand, the bowl of a large wooden spoon, or a burnisher. Set the container aside to dry for a week.

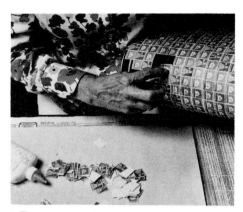

6: To cover a container with stamps, decoupage style, work from top to bottom as you glue each stamp in place individually. If the container has square corners, let the stamps wrap around them.

7: Brush a light coat of clear varnish over the stamps on the outside of the container and over lining paper if you use any. Varnish will protect them. Let the varnish dry before continuing.

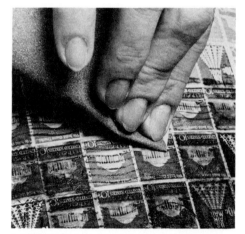

8: With fine sandpaper, lightly rub the container to smooth the varnish and prepare it for the next coat. Remove sanding dust between applications of varnish. You need to apply from six to ten coats to build up a good layer of protection.

9: Glue ribbon, rickrack, or braiding around the rim and perhaps the base of the container. Pull the trim tautly as you wrap, and let it overlap slightly at any joint. When the glue is dry, cut through the joint so ends meet precisely.

Varnishing and Trim

To preserve the stamps and keep them from peeling off, seal them with six to ten coats of clear varnish. Varnish comes in yellow and orange tones to simulate antique finishes, but I find these obscure the beautiful colors of the stamps, so I prefer clear varnish. The sealing procedure is time-consuming because you must sand the container lightly with fine sandpaper or fine steel wool after each coat of varnish is dry. I use a fast-drying varnish that is now available at many craft shops.

Cover your work surface with newspapers. Tilt the container on its side, and apply a coat of varnish inside and out (photograph 7). When the varnish is dry, rub the surface lightly with fine sandpaper (photograph 8) and wipe away the sanding dust with a rag dampened with turpentine. If the dust is trapped between coats of varnish, it builds up stubbly areas. Apply another coat of varnish. Repeat until the surface is as smooth and shiny as you can make it.

Trimming the container is largely a matter of personal taste; you may not feel the need for any at all. Sewing centers and variety stores stock a wide variety of notions for decorative borders. To apply a band of ribbon or braid to the edge of a container, start by cutting a strip or strips to fit. Leave an extra ¼ inch at any joint. Spread white glue on the back of the ribbon or braid. Then apply the trim to the container just below its rim (photograph 9). Let the glue dry; use a vertical cut to remove excess trim at a joint so the ends abut precisely.

For related projects see the entries: "Boxes," "Collages and Assemblages," "Decoupage," "Greeting Cards," and "Mosaics."

STENCILING
Ornamenting With Ingenuity

Betty Carrie teaches colonial crafts in her studio home, The Hammock, in Florham Park, New Jersey. In addition to teaching stenciling, she gives expert instruction in crewel embroidery, needlepoint, and rug hooking. She operates a mail-order business selling craft kits featuring her needlework and stencil designs. She also demonstrates colonial craft skills at The Crane House, a museum in Montclair, New Jersey.

Stenciling is a basic art technique that you can use to put designs on many surfaces, including paper, fabric, metal, plaster, wallboard, and wood. A stenciler places a cutout pattern on the surface to be decorated and fills the cutout with paint or ink. With this simple decorating tool, a design can be repeated as many times as seems desirable to produce a heavily ornamented effect.

The term, stencil, is apparently derived from the old French *estanceler*—to sparkle or to be covered with stars—which in turn comes from the Latin *stincilla* or *scintilla*, meaning a spark. As a decorative technique, stenciling has been used sporadically through the centuries. Examples of stenciling exist from many civilizations. It was highly developed by the ancient Egyptians and in Oriental cultures; 2,000 years ago the Chinese, who are believed to have invented the technique, used stencils with results that contemporary stencilers envy.

The craft became popular in America soon after the Revolution. It was used to imitate costly products such as inlaid furniture and hand painted wallpaper. Stenciling also provided a practical way to ornament an otherwise drab object. Furniture and tinware decorated with stenciled designs were especially popular. But as industrialization progressed, stenciling all but disappeared, giving way to faster machine methods. Between 1900 and 1940 stenciling reappeared in public buildings, then lapsed again into obsolescence. It is now the object of renewed interest as a fine applied art.

You do not need to be an artist to use stencils with a flair. When you have mastered the projects pictured here for stenciling paper and fabric, you will be ready to begin more demanding stencil work on walls, ceilings, and floors. Then you can make use of the full-sized patterns (opposite and on pages 2244 and 2246) in projects of your own choice. You will also find that stenciling can be done effectively within a very limited budget.

For centuries Japanese used stencils to decorate fabrics worn by both men and women. The designs were often so delicate that a large, soft brush was used to apply the paint so the artist could avoid tearing the fragile paper.

Figure A: Ever since the first stencil was devised, stenciling has been used as a decorating technique throughout the world. This sampler of stencil designs shows how varied the styles have been; they are shown full size so you can trace and adapt them to your own stenciling needs. The chrysanthemum at the top is a Japanese design; the griffin and the swan are Victorian and the others are Early American.

A

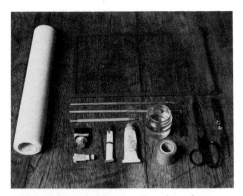

1: Materials needed for stencil work are freezer paper (left); oil paints; pencil; artist's paint-brushes; turpentine; single-edged razor blades; masking tape; scissors; palette knife; and (top right) a pane of glass to cut on.

Materials

You will need a piece of window glass approximately 8 by 10 inches to use as a surface for cutting stencils. Wrap the glass edges with masking tape or cloth tape to forestall cuts from glass splinters and sharp edges. Other supplies needed include: a medium-soft lead pencil; masking tape; scissors; tubes of artist's oil paints; palette knife; paint thinner or turpentine; several stipple or stencil brushes (artist's brushes called brights can be substituted); single-edged razor blades; and stencil paper (photograph 1). If paper made especially for stencils is not available, the paper sold in supermarkets as freezer wrap is an excellent substitute and is usually less expensive. In some cases, regular stencil paper stretches out of shape after numerous uses, whereas freezer wrap stays in shape longer. I advise my students to check available supplies at home before buying any materials. Specialized stenciling equipment is usually available at art-supply stores, toy and hobby shops, and at some hardware stores. If stenciling supplies are unavailable in your area, you can order them by mail from:

American Decorative Arts, Inc., Box 117, Dorset, Vt. 05251
Betty Carrie, Ltd., Box 39, Florham Park, N. J. 07932
Macmillan Arts & Crafts, Inc., 9520 Baltimore Ave., College Park, Md. 20740
Sax Arts and Crafts, 207 Milwaukee St., Milwaukee, Wisc. 53202

Cutting a Stencil

Because stencil cutting requires a bit of a knack, practice on scrap stencil paper. First select a design from Figure D, page 2245, or use a design of your own devising that has clean, simple lines. Do not hesitate to borrow designs from magazines, gift-wrap paper, children's coloring books, or commercial packaging. Plan the design so the stencil paper is more than 1 inch larger on each edge than the design (photograph 2). Keep your fingers clean and your work neat. Trace the design onto stencil paper (photograph 3).

Any small table such as a card table provides an adequate work space for cutting the stencil; the top will be protected by the piece of glass. Put the stencil-paper tracing on the glass; study the design before you begin to cut. Always cut the smaller parts of the design first (leaves, stems, centers); then cut the large areas. Otherwise, the stencil will become too lacy to hold firmly as you cut small parts of the design.

With a single-edged razor blade held in your writing hand, put light pressure on the blade to make the first cut. (Often beginners get tense and either break the corner of the blade or scratch the glass with too much pressure.) Then, with your other hand, slowly rotate the stencil paper, following the design clockwise if you are right-handed, so you can always see the entire shape of the piece being cut. When you come to a sharp corner, tilt the razor's edge up to make the point of contact as tiny as possible; this forestalls tearing as you pivot the stencil with the other hand. Once you start cutting the stencil paper, do not lift the razor blade until you have completed that portion of the design (photograph 4). (I pretend I am using a sewing machine, and I move the paper with my free hand as if it were fabric.)

2: A stencil should have substantial margins all around (as do these) to keep your work neat. These stencils were made for use on walls and ceiling (top) and on place mats (bottom).

3: Draw your full-size stencil design; then trace it onto a piece of freezer paper cut to the size you need. The freezer paper will be cut to form the actual stencil plate.

4: Cut the smaller openings of the stencil first, using very light pressure on the razor blade. Do not lift the blade until an opening has been cut all around. Pivot the paper when you reach a corner.

Figure B: By enlarging this alphabet, you can make a stencil that you can use to label any large object, even one made of fabric like the knapsack pictured on page 2247. Copy the letters, square by square, on paper that you have ruled in ¼-inch squares. To obtain the letter O, omit the tail on the letter Q.

1 square = ¼ inch

CINNAMON

CLOVES

ALLSPICE

NUTMEGS

GINGER

MACE

C
Figure C: If you enjoy stenciling on paper, try tracing and cutting some of these full-sized designs for spice-jar labels. To protect the finished labels, coat them with clear plastic spray or clear nail polish.

A simple elegance marks these four basic one-color designs that have a variety of hearts and flowers suggested for decorating personal note paper.

Designs and Decorations
Personalized notes

The oldest examples of stenciling on paper include playing cards and religious pictures, known as image prints, dating from the fourteenth century. A modern application is pictured above, hand-decorated notepaper made with stencils that reflect both stylized and traditional designs. Patterns like these are easy to use in making personal stationery, unique gifts, or bazaar wares. With stencils, you can turn used grocery bags into very special wrapping paper. Other uses for interesting but easy stenciling include party invitations, banquet decorations, and home-canning or spice-jar labels (left).

Materials
For stenciling on paper, you will need the materials listed on page 2242 plus the stationery or other paper you wish to decorate. I use a facial tissue, rather than a brush, to apply the artist's oil paints to the paper. It makes the clean-up a snap, for the tissue goes into the wastebasket. You can use undiluted acrylic paints instead of oils, but I prefer oils because they are easier to apply; acrylics must be applied with a brush. Broad, felt-tipped pens also work for stenciling on paper.

D

Figure D: To make a stencil for stationery, choose one of these full-sized patterns to trace onto the freezer paper that you will cut.

Stenciling

To begin, select one of the full-sized designs shown in Figure D. Following the directions on page 2242, trace the design onto stencil paper; then carefully cut it out to make the stencil plate. For fast, accurate production, mark the stencil plate to indicate the exact position for the top edge and corners of the paper being stenciled. You will be able to see through the translucent stencil as you slip the paper under it (photograph 5). To arrive at a paint color you like, you may need to mix two colors. The red used to stencil the heart-and-brushstroke motif pictured is a mixture of yellow ocher and vermillion. I use a small piece of paper as a mixing palette for oils (photograph 6), but a square of glass or a piece of taped-down aluminum foil would work as well. Practice blending various colors until you determine how to achieve shades pleasing to you.

For applying oils to paper, I use a facial tissue folded in quarters and wrapped around my forefinger (photograph 7). In effect, I am staining the paper rather than painting it. This minimizes the danger of smearing the paint. Regular stencil brushes or stipple brushes sometimes tear the paper. Experiment on scrap paper, using circular motions, up-and-down strokes, or any other technique you find effective in achieving a smooth, even finish. For large cutouts, apply paint at the outer edges first, working in toward the center. Apply the paint sparingly. When the design is filled in, let the paint set for a few seconds before removing the piece of stationery. You can lift the stencil plate if you like, of course, but that means untaping one end. Instead, gently slide the finished paper away from you by pushing on the bottom edge. If the paint is not too thick the paper will slide through without smearing. Oils require drying time. Spread the stationery out without overlapping until the paint is dry.

5: Mark the stencil plate to indicate where the paper should be positioned for stenciling. Then tape the plate down and slide the paper under it until it matches the marked lines.

6: Use your forefinger wrapped in facial tissue to work a small amount of oil paint on a freezer-paper palette until it reaches a smooth, evenly mixed consistency.

7: Coat the cutout area of the stencil plate with paint, dabbing on small amounts with a tissue-covered finger. Finish painting an entire element of the design before moving on to the next one.

E

Figure E: After you have cut a few stencils, try this more difficult design. It is shown full size so you can trace it directly onto stencil paper.

The geometric design stenciled on this place mat is at home in any setting, be it traditional or modern. These motifs can be applied along just one edge of the fabric, as pictured, or they can march single-file around the border of a tablecloth, sheet, pillow case, or drapery.

Designs and Decorations

Dressed-up place mats

Stenciling can change almost any fabric from plain to fancy at little cost. This technique of fabric decoration has long been used. In sixteenth-century France, for example, the devoutly religious carried stenciled banners on their pilgrimages.

If you want to decorate household fabrics, consider the colors already in the rooms where they will be used. The place mat pictured above has colors that go well with those in the wallpaper in my kitchen, but they also complement the colors in the dining room, so they can be used in either room. For family fun, you can adapt these fabric-stenciling techniques to decorate camping gear (opposite), T-shirts, scarves, or handkerchiefs. Once you become adept at fabric stenciling, you can try using more complex designs such as the one in Figure E.

Materials

To stencil fabric, you will need the materials listed on page 2242, but you will use oil-based textile paint, extender base, and solvent instead of artist's oils and turpentine. To set the paint so it won't wash out, you also need an iron and pressing cloth. You will need masking tape to hold the fabric in place and a drawing board or breadboard to use as a work surface. Most fabrics are quite easy to stencil. Wool is difficult, however; test a scrap before you try to stencil anything made of wool. With other fibers, for best results select white or pastel fabric. To make eight of the place mats shown, start with two yards of 44-inch-wide homespun cotton.

Preparing the Fabric

Wash the fabric to remove any sizing; then rinse and dry. If you are using a fabric that requires dry cleaning, have that done before proceeding. Iron the cloth to remove wrinkles. To make the place mats pictured, cut the fabric into eight rectangles, each 16 by 20 inches. Make a ½-inch fringe all around each mat; then machine-stitch inside the fringe to prevent further raveling.

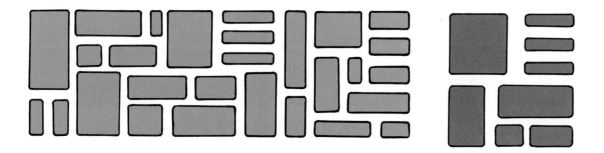

F

Figure F: To make stencil plates for the place mat pictured opposite, trace these designs directly onto stencil paper, making a separate stencil for each color. Then cut out along the outlines.

Stenciling

Transfer the full-sized designs (Figure F) to stencil paper and cut out the stencil (page 2242). I put newspapers under the article I'm stenciling so the paper will absorb any paint that soaks through the fabric. For stenciling, stretch the fabric smoothly over the work surface and either tape it or tack it down if you wish. On small pieces such as the place mat, use the threads of the fabric as a guide in positioning the stencil plate. Place the first place mat motif 1½ inches in from the edge of the side of the fabric. Apply each subsequent motif ¾ inch from the previous motif.

Oil-based textile paints come with a liquid medium (known as extender base) that dilutes the colors and makes them permanent. Thoroughly stir both the paint and the extender base before you mix them together. Use a palette knife to take up small amounts of extender and paint, placing them on a taped-down square of freezer paper (your palette). Then mix the extender and the color or colors selected (photograph 8). Always add color to the extender, not the reverse. You can mix several colors together, if you like, to brighten or soften shades.

To apply the paint to a fabric, use a flat stipple brush or a bright brush held in a vertical position (photograph 9). (It is most convenient to have a separate brush for each color.) Take up a tiny amount of paint and apply it to the fabric, working from the outside edges of the cutout to its center. When you finish stenciling, let the paint get thoroughly dry. This takes at least 24 hours. Clean your brushes with textile-paint solvent after each use. You should also use the solvent on the stencil, if you plan to use it again. When the paint is dry, set it with a hot iron to make the design permanent and washable. Iron the fabric design-side up, covering it with a dry cloth and pressing from three to five minutes at a moderate setting. Adjust the temperature to suit the fabric, keeping in mind that with lower heat, more time is required to cure the paints.

Camping equipment such as this canvas backpack takes on a military air when a name is applied with the help of a stencil.

8: Prepare textile paint for use by mixing it into an extender base that makes the color permanent. If an article will be laundered infrequently, the extender base may be eliminated.

9: To apply textile paint through a stencil, hold the brush vertically. Pick up a small amount of paint and make dabbing strokes, working from the outside toward the center of the cutout.

An unusual effect results from two-tone stenciling, used to create a mirrored look on light walls and a dark ceiling. The close-up (inset) shows a well-planned corner.

Designs and Decorations
Fancy-paint walls and ceilings $ ◑ ⚐ ✈

Stenciled walls, once called fancy painting, were in vogue in the early part of the nineteenth century. They were usually executed by itinerant painters. Designs ranged from simple borders to very intricate schemes. A bedroom for honey-mooners might have a hearts-and-flowers border. A patriot might use liberty-bell or eagle designs. Sometimes several patterns had related colors that linked rooms throughout the house. At first, stenciling was used primarily to make geometric borders. Later entire walls were stenciled with stylized fruits and flowers. Stenciled walls appeared primarily in New England and the Middle Atlantic states; they boomed briefly, then were replaced by a newer craze—wallpaper.

Today, the pendulum has swung again, for anyone can have wallpaper. But stenciling can give you an individualized, one-of-a-kind look in a wall treatment for a kitchen, bathroom, or nursery. In a living-dining area or a bedroom, stenciled borders can be made to look like expensive architectural moldings. Simple spot designs are effective on ceilings where a continuous design might make a room seem over-decorated.

Materials
In addition to the materials listed on page 2242, you will need a half-dozen squares (approximately 4 by 4 inches) of velour for applying the paint, an aluminum pie plate, and a stepladder. If you use an oil-base paint, you may want to cut your stencil from architect's linen, a more expensive material available at art-supply stores, though I used freezer wrap for stenciling the small room pictured above. I prefer fast-drying, flat-finish oil for wall stenciling. But you may wish to experiment with water-based paints such as latex or casein.

Preparation
Before walls are stenciled, they must be properly prepared. Remove any nails, fill holes with spackling compound, let it dry, and sand smooth. You may need to wash and paint the walls. I washed off fingerprints and scuff marks, retouched where necessary, and began to stencil.

1 square = ¼ inch

G

Figure G: To enlarge the pattern used on the stenciled walls and ceiling pictured opposite, copy it, square by square, on paper that you have ruled in ¼-inch squares. Follow the lines of the design as you transfer it to the larger grid.

You will need to make two stencil plates, one for each color. Enlarge the pattern (Figure G). Then trace the pattern onto two pieces of stencil paper and cut them out (page 2242). Before beginning to stencil, measure the surface you intend to stencil and plan the design to fit it. If, for instance, the wall is 10 feet long and the stencil pattern is 12 inches long, you will be able to place nine repeats on the wall and have 6 inches left on either end for a corner design. If you are using the same pattern on both walls and ceilings, as I did, you must decide in advance where you want to match the design and how you will fill the wall corners, remembering that the ceiling border is shorter than the wall border. To allow for this difference, do the corner stenciling last.

Stenciling
Pour a small amount of stenciling paint into an aluminum pie pan, attached to the stepladder tray with masking tape. Position the stencil plate to the right of one ceiling corner, as determined by your plan, and hold it there with masking tape. Wrap your forefinger with a velour square and take up a very small amount of paint. Fill in the cutout areas of the stencil, doing the border brushstroke shapes first, the stems and small cutouts next, finally filling in the larger areas. Begin at the outside edges of the larger openings, working toward the centers. To keep the paint from creeping under the stencil plate, hold it flat against the surface, and apply paint very sparingly. Let the paint set momentarily; then remove the stencil. Check the design carefully, and retouch it with an artist's brush if necessary. Then check the back of the stencil plate and clean off any paint smudges before you place it against the wall again to apply the next motifs. Working from left to right, finish stenciling the ceiling along the first side. Continue around the ceiling perimeter, skipping the corners. Then, still leaving out the corners, repeat the process on the walls, matching the positions of the designs on the ceiling. Finally, select those parts of the design that line up best—flower to flower—for the corners. When rounding the corners, first fill in the brushstroke motifs that border this design; then adjust the pattern to get a suitable design in the middle sections. The borders on the stencil plate are your guideline for aligning the stencil. If you use the design vertically on a wall, locate a true vertical by hanging a weighted plumb line from the ceiling as close to the adjacent wall as possible. Mark that line with chalk or a pencil, and follow it when you position the stencil.

The vines of this stenciled motif seem to twine across the floor of a gift shop, Daisy Two, in Florham Park, New Jersey. Only one stencil was used, but it called for two shades of green painted on an off-white background.

Designs and Decorations
Focus on floors

Nearly a century before stenciled walls came into vogue, stenciled floors were under foot. By the early 1800s country housewives in the U. S. had worked out ways to mimic costly floor coverings by stenciling. The museum floor pictured opposite, duplicating a floor stencil painted around the year 1820, is typical of early geometric designs. In sharp contrast is the modern leaf pattern on the floor shown above. This design is made from a single stylized stencil of a branch, calling for two colors of paint.

Materials
In addition to the materials listed on page 2242, you will need a commercial wood filler; sandpaper; oil-based primer; floor paint and varnish, paintbrushes; several 6-inch squares of velour (for applying the paint) and polyurethane finish to protect the stenciled design.

Floor Preparation
The procedures used to produce these floors are similar to the techniques used for walls and ceilings (pages 2248 and 2249). A smooth, clean, freshly painted surface is needed to achieve a good finished product. Fill any nail holes or other mars with a commercial wood filler. Sand the floor smooth, wipe it to remove all sanding dust, and scrub it if necessary. Then give the floor time to dry.

Apply a coat of primer in the desired color and let it dry. Apply a coat of oil-based floor paint, adding ½ pint of varnish to 1 gallon of paint to toughen the finish. Let the paint get thoroughly dry before you begin the stencil.

Stenciling
Select one of the designs for floor stencils shown in Figures H and I; enlarge it, and transfer it to freezer paper. If you are using more than one color, you can cut a separate stencil for each color. But if your design is large enough to keep the colors well separated, a single stencil can be used for speed and perfect register.

Make the stencil (page 2242). Then plan how the floor will be decorated. The ar-

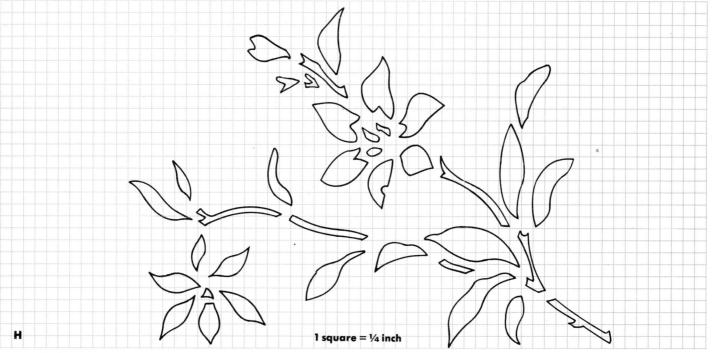

Figure H: To enlarge this pattern for the vine design pictured opposite, copy it, square by square, onto paper that you have ruled into ¼-inch squares.

Staff members of the Museum of Early Trades and Crafts in Madison, New Jersey, carefully painted this laurel-leaf-and-flower-petal wreath, a replica of an Early American design.

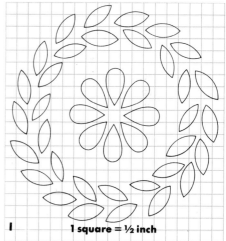

Figure I: To make this pattern for the geometric wreath motif pictured at left, copy the design, square by square, onto paper that you have ruled into ½-inch squares.

rangement of the motifs will be determined by the design and the position of furniture in the room. The wreath pattern is geometric, so it suggests a formal arrangement with uniform spacing. The branch design has a more casual feeling, and is appropriate for a random, free-flowing placement.

Position the stencil (page 2249). Apply the paint to the cutouts, using a square of velour wrapped around your forefinger. When you finish stenciling, let the paint dry for several days. Then apply one or more coats of polyurethane floor finish to protect the design, letting it dry between coats.

For related crafts, see "Linoleum and Woodcuts" and "Supergraphics."

STONE PAINTING
Rock Fans

Stones smoothed by the tumbling action of rushing water in river or surf offer an inviting surface for painted decorations. Since the surface of a stone is nonabsorbent, applied colors never appear washed out or faded as they sometimes do on paper. Almost any kind of paint can be used. I generally use water-based paint, especially when I am working with children, because the cleanup is so easy. But I have experimented with oils as well, and they work too. Oils are more durable than watercolors and other water-based paints, but the latter can be protected from wear or weathering with several coats of clear polyurethane varnish. Depending on the shape and size of the stones you collect, you may want to convert them into jewelry with jewelry findings, as in the key-chain fob on page 2255. Or you may want to glue them together with epoxy cement to make amusing assemblages, as in the frog on page 2257. But there is no reason why a painted stone cannot be enjoyed simply for its own sake, as any art object.

We're Off
With a pail in each hand, my son Chris and I comb neighboring beaches, but we collect stones rather than seashells. Surf-polished white and gray stones that contain a great deal of quartz are abundant. When we have gathered as much as our pails can hold or we can carry, we head for home to clean our treasures. We wash the stones by spreading them on the lawn, sprinkling on a small amount of powdered soap, and spraying them with the garden hose. Using a soft bristle brush, we can remove any stubborn dirt or moss. Then we rinse the stones and let them dry in the sun before we take them indoors for sorting by size and shape.

June Lepore of Brooklyn, New York, was graduated from the University of Maryland with a degree in theater arts. After graduation, she joined a summer theater group in Maryland. A parking lot near the theater was surfaced with smooth stones, prompting her to paint them and hand them out as opening-night gifts. The show was a hit and so were the gifts.

Designs and Decorations
Creative assemblages   ¢ ☒ 👫 🔥

Given watercolors and brushes, children will doodle feverishly on any stone in sight. And you will find some of their designs enchanting (right). But for a more ambitious undertaking, you can show a small child how to put together a simple stone bird or animal that he can then decorate in any way he pleases—from cuddly creature to mad monster.

To make the penguin pictured dancing on a picnic table far from the wilds of Antarctica (page 2254) you will need two rather flat, oblong stones for the feet, and a larger flat, oval stone for the body. (The feet must be of the same thickness for the body to balance properly.) In addition, you will need: fine sandpaper; a sheet of plastic wrap or a plastic bag; two-part quick-drying epoxy cement; toothpicks; a scrap of cardboard; watercolor, tempera, or water-based acrylic paints; artist's paintbrushes; and a container of water.

Examine each stone for grease spots that could keep paint or glue from adhering. You can remove such spots from most stones by rubbing them lightly with fine sandpaper. Cover the work surface with a sheet of plastic, and arrange the stone feet in a V shape with the back edges touching. Following the directions on the gluing tubes, mix a little two-part epoxy on a scrap of cardboard with a toothpick. (One of the tubes contains an activator; mix only what you can use immediately and work quickly so you finish before the mixture hardens.) Apply epoxy between the inner back edges of the feet (photograph 1, page 2254). Any excess glue will peel off the plastic but adhere to the stones when dry, so you can use the glue like a filler to enlarge the glued area. This provides a more stable stand.

You would look twice if you came upon these painted stones in a garden. The larger ones make handsome paperweights as well as indoor or outdoor garden decorations; the smaller stones could be incorporated in jewelry designs.

If you give children watercolors, paintbrushes, and an assortment of stones, you may start a neighborhood hobby. If rocks painted with watercolors are protected with clear polyurethane varnish, the designs will stay bright for years.

When this glue is dry, balance the wider edge of the body stone on the feet where they are glued. When the balance point is found, mix more epoxy and apply it between the body and the feet (photograph 2). Press together for a few minutes; then set the assemblage aside until the glue hardens. To decorate the stone, follow the full-sized pattern for the penguin (Figure A). Use a pencil to draw the outlines of the pattern on the stone. Then use paints to fill in the colors shown. Depending on the age of the children, you might find it more fun—and certainly more stimulating to the imagination—to glue stones together into figure shapes; then let the children create their own fantasy creatures.

A

Figure A: Use a pencil to scribe two arcs for the wings of a penguin. Line up the midpoint of the eyes with the top edges of the wings. Center a beak just below the eyes, and finish with a dapper bow tie. Heart shapes can be drawn over the feet for flippers.

From rocks, glue, and paint, fantasy creatures can be created. Here, June and Chris are painting pompous-looking penguins with big feet.

1: To make feet for a stone creature, place two oblong stones of the same thickness and approximate size in a V shape on a sheet of plastic. Use a toothpick to dab epoxy cement between the stones to hold them together.

2: Center, balance, then glue an oval-shaped stone body over the glued area of the feet. Any excess glue that runs between the feet will enlarge the stand, since the hardened glue will not stick to the plastic.

Jewelry, Lapidary and Metalwork
Key-chain fob
¢ ▣ 👥 🔥

A small, flat stone can be decorated, then hung from a key chain (such as the one pictured at right) or from a choker ring to make a necklace like the one I am wearing in the photograph opposite. Designs such as flowers, fruits, vegetables, animals, zodiac signs, or hex signs lend themselves to this use. An assortment of jeweler's findings, useful in making rings, earrings, or necklaces, can be ordered from any

3: Guided by a pencil sketch, use a drawing pen or a pointed felt-tipped marker to darken the design so the edges will stand out crisply after the paint is applied.

4: Using acrylic paints (above) or watercolors, fill in the inked design. Thin acrylic paint slightly with water if that is needed to make it flow smoothly onto the surface of the stone.

Small, decorated stones, such as this one displaying plump strawberries, can be attached to key rings and necklace chains with jeweler's findings, in this case a bell cap and a jump ring.

jewelry craft supplier. But to attach a painted stone to a key chain, you need only a bell cap and a jump ring.

In addition, you will need: a jeweler's pliers; a small, light colored, oval-shaped rock; pencil; technical drawing pen or pointed felt-tipped marker with permanent ink; two-part epoxy cement; toothpicks; cardboard; ice-cube tray; watercolors or acrylic paints; artist's paintbrushes; containers of water; polyurethane varnish; turpentine; large paper clips; coat hanger; newspapers; clear cellophane tape; sandpaper; and rags.

Use a pencil to sketch your design on the face of the stone; you can follow the full-sized strawberry pattern (Figure B) if you like. Then darken the pencil lines with a drawing pen or felt-tipped marker (photograph 3); you want these lines to show. Once the ink is dry, fill in the design with paint (photograph 4). To make acrylic paint flow easily onto a stone, you may need to thin it a bit with water. When the paint is dry, fit the prongs of a bell cap snugly over the center of the stone's top edge (photograph 5, page 2256). Use a toothpick to mix the two-part epoxy on cardboard and to apply it to the inside of the bell cap and the top of the stone.

Press the bell cap in place, and set the stone upright in an ice-cube tray until the glue sets. Use jeweler's (or needle-nosed) pliers to open a jump ring just enough to slide it through the loop on the bell cap. Then close the ends of the jump ring. (When you glue stones to earring backings or ring findings, lightly sand both surfaces being joined so the epoxy can get a good grip.)

To keep a design from wearing off a stone, cover it with four coats of polyurethane varnish. Protect the work surface with newspapers. (You can clean up any splashes with turpentine or benzene.) The easiest way to coat a stone evenly is to dip it in polyurethane. Make a dipping and drying hook by pulling a large paper clip apart. Slide the jump ring over one end of the paper clip. With the stone dangling, dip it in the polyurethane (photograph 6, page 2256). Coat the jump ring and bell cap as well to keep them from tarnishing. Let excess polyurethane drain back into the can and remove the droplet at the bottom with a toothpick. Then tape the paper clip to the edge of a shelf while the sealer dries.

When you dip several stones at once, hang them on a wire coat hanger. When

B

Figure B: Sketch this pair of strawberries with flowery caps, stems, and leaves in the middle of any round stone. Draw dashed lines on each berry to give it shape and texture.

2255

5: Before gluing, fit a bell-cap finding to the stone's shape. Findings with a very smooth, shiny surface will be easier to cement to the stone if both joining surfaces are roughened slightly with fine sandpaper.

6: Bend a paper clip so you can hook the jump ring onto it. Then dunk the stone, finding and all, in polyurethane varnish. Use a toothpick to remove the droplet that forms at the bottom of the stone as it drains.

7: Between each of the four coats of polyurethane varnish needed to protect the design, let the finish dry; then rub it gently with fine sandpaper or steel wool. This keeps the finish smooth and even. Wipe the stone to remove dust before each dipping.

the polyurethane is dry, rub the stone lightly with fine sandpaper or fine steel wool (photograph 7). Smoothing between coats ensures a smooth, glossy surface, but you must wipe any sanding dust from the stone before you apply the next coat of finish. Dust with a rag dipped in turpentine. Repeat dippings, sandings, and dustings until the stone has four coats of polyurethane. Do not sand the final coat. Then attach the key chain to the jump ring on the stone.

Designs and Decorations
Caricatures in stone

C
Figure C: If you like, you can trace this owl; then use carbon paper to transfer the image onto a smooth, light-colored stone. Ink the lines on the stone with a felt-tipped marker. To draw your own owl, start with two small ovals atop a larger one. Use arcs for wings, U shapes for feathers, narrow ovals for claws.

To create a freestanding sculpture like this one, you will need a stable branch of driftwood. Cement the painted stones to the wood, making sure you do not disturb the balance of the piece. Then coat the stones with polyurethane varnish. Since the piece will not be handled, it is not necessary to sand the varnish.

With imagination, amusing caricatures of the birds and the beasts can be created by painting stones—like the morose frog pictured below, right, and the flock of wise old owls pictured opposite. To make your own animal character, you first must find a rock that somewhat resembles the shape of that animal. I chose oval stones for the owls perched on the branch of driftwood. But for the body of a frog about to hop, I had to find a large, teardrop-shaped stone. To this I added two small, oval stones on which to paint the frog's bulging eyes. Extra stones could just as well be glued on a body to make a squirrel's tail or an alligator's feet.

Materials

To make an animal sculpture, you need: a pencil; two-part epoxy cement; toothpicks; cardboard; clear cellophane tape; absorbent cotton or cotton string; watercolors or acrylic paints; artist's paintbrushes; a container of water; newspapers; polyurethane varnish; a ¼-inch nylon paintbrush; sandpaper; turpentine; and rags.

Fastening Features

When you have found the right stone, decide where the top and bottom should be. Set the stone in its planned position to make sure that it can be balanced that way. Then, in pencil, sketch the design on the exposed surfaces of the stone. If you like, you can use the drawing of a frog in Figure D or of the owl in Figure C, opposite, as a guide. To add three-dimensional features such as the frog's eyes, position the smaller stones and mark their location with the pencil. Mix epoxy cement and use a toothpick to spread it over the marks (photograph 8). Glue the small stones in place. Since the point of contact may be very small, clamp the stones in place with two strips of clear cellophane tape. Remove the tape when the epoxy has hardened; then strengthen the joint by wrapping it with absorbent cotton or a bit of cotton string saturated with epoxy cement (photograph 9). Set aside to dry.

Painting the Caricature

An effective caricature has a minimum of lines, exaggerating the most distinctive features. When you are satisfied with your pencil sketch, darken the lines with a drawing pen or sharp felt-tipped marker. Then paint in the design with the colors you have chosen, either realistic or ridiculous. I gave Freddy, the frog shown in the color photograph at right, a wild paint job. I applied bright yellow paint over his stomach; then I covered his green back with a black and yellow polka-dot design. You might like to paint small flowers, pussy willows, or grass along the bottom edge of the stone to give the frog a natural setting. When the paint is dry, brush a coat of clear polyurethane varnish over the top of the stone. Once this dries, turn the stone over and cover the bottom the same way. Sanding lightly and dusting carefully between coats, apply at least six coats of polyurethane. These amusing critters can be used to decorate indoor or outdoor gardens. The polyurethane makes the decorations impervious to water.

For related entries, see "Beachcombing" and "Seashells."

D
Figure D: This frog drawing starts with the inverted triangle that becomes the body; the head fits in a rectangle centered on top of the triangle. Draw the frog freehand, or trace this pattern. Cattails or other swamp plants provide a simple setting.

This stone frog has been out in the rain; but its paint, including the teardrop, is protected by several layers of glossy polyurethane varnish.

8: The outline of a frog has been sketched on this teardrop-shaped stone; now smaller stones are being cemented onto the top edge for eyes.

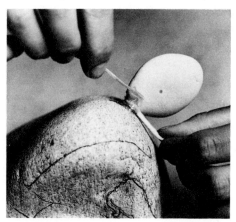

9: To strengthen the joint between stones, saturate a thin strip of absorbent cotton in epoxy and wrap it around the joint.

STREET GAMES
Free Play

Richard Griffin ran for his high school track team, but he also played street games such as skullies, follow-the-leader, association football, stickball, and basketball as a child in East Harlem, New York. He received a master's degree in guidance and psychological services from Springfield College in Massachusetts. He is a guidance counselor for the Boy's Club of New York, advising families as well as boys. When he is not acting as a tutor for the Youth Corps and organizing recreational activities for the Boy's Club, Richard enjoys writing poetry and listening to jazz.

Fudge, fudge, call the judge. Johnny-on-the-pony, one-two-three. If these phrases are foreign to you, chances are you have never played street games—games like kick-the-can, jump rope, ring-a-levio, and Johnny-on-the-pony. These games, and others like them, have thrilled generations of youngsters who grew up in cities. Lacking the room required for many traditional sports, city kids came up with satisfying adaptations of the games all youngsters love—just how satisfying can be seen opposite where youngsters are playing Johnny-on-the-pony, a vigorous form of team leapfrog. It can collapse a group of youngsters into giggles, develop muscles, and build quite a bit of team spirit. (How can you not feel team spirit if the fellow next to you is supporting half the weight of someone sitting on your back?)

Some street games are easy to trace. Stickball is a direct descendent of baseball. In baseball, you have a fairly heavy bat to wield but in stickball, a thin broom handle is a greater challenge; you are playing a whole new ball game. Association football is a similar case. It is the child of football, but because a tag of the hands replaces tackling, the adaptation is particularly good for small children.

Street games like association, stickball, and Johnny-on-the-pony are described and demonstrated on the following pages. There are 15 games in all, and they range from vigorous body-contact sports to skilled aiming games and not-so-traditional jump-rope games. Although the games are shown on city streets, where they originated, they are just as much fun played in a field, on a school playground, or, in bad weather, in a school gym. These games are almost infinitely adaptable to the number of youngsters, to the age of the players, and to the space available.

Toys and Games
Johnny-on-the-pony

Pitting a jumping team against a pony team, Johnny-on-the-pony is the classic street game. Members of the pony team form a chain by bending over and locking hands around waists (opposite). The members of the other team leapfrog onto (not over) this pony. For the jumpers to be victorious, they must break the chain.

Since Johnny-on-the-pony is a rough-and-tumble game, use teams of at least five players of approximately the same size and weight. The game is played in front of a wall, tree, or pole. The teams take turns jumping, with the first jumper determined by any "choose" listed in the box on page 2261. One member of the pony team is chosen to be the pillow. He stands erect with his back against the wall or pole to support and brace his team members during the game. The others assume the pony position, forming a straight line facing the pillow. Each member of the pony team bends at the waist and wraps his arms around the waist of the team member directly in front of him, locking his fingers together and tucking his chin toward his chest to avoid being jolted or kicked by the jumpers. Each member of the jumping team gets one chance to vault onto the pony. The first jumper must vault the farthest in order to land near the pillow and leave room for his teammates. To vault, a jumper runs, presses both hands on the lower back of the end pony, and, as he jumps, pushes himself forward. A jump is concluded when all members of the jumping team have had one turn. Then the pillow must say three times, "Johnny-on-the-pony, one-two-three." If the pony collapses at any time during the jump, the jumping team scores one point. The pony team scores if any man jumping touches the ground before the jump ends. If neither team scores, the game is a tie and is resolved by allowing one more jump per team until a winner is determined.

One of the most popular of street games is an elaborate form of team leapfrog known as Johnny-on-the-pony. The member of the pony team in the pillow position, leaning against the wall, cushions the head of the pony and absorbs the jolt of the leap. Here, pony-team members break into fits of laughter because the jumper left very little room for his four teammates waiting their turns to pile on.

Skullies

1: As many as six kids can play a game of skullies. To start, each player in turn sets his loady, (a bottle cap filled with clay) anywhere behind the outline of the skullies square and aims the loady at box No. 13. The player whose loady comes the closest to box No. 13 gets the first turn to aim for box No. 1 located at a corner of the skullies square. If his loady lands in box No. 1 he continues to box No. 2. But if he misses he must wait until his next turn.

Skullies is a target game vaguely resembling marbles, in that aim and strategy count the most. It is played in boxes chalked on a hard surface—pavement or blacktop (photographs 1 and 2). Boxes are numbered from one through 13. The object of the game is to flick a playing piece, called a loady, into each box, progressing from one to another in numerical order.

From two to six players can join in a game of skullies. They may play singly or in pairs. Each player makes a loady by filling a soda-bottle cap with clay, then letting the clay bake in the sun until it hardens. To set up the game, use chalk to draw a 5-foot skullies court on a smooth spot of pavement, following Figure A. Then mark each box within the large square with the proper number.

Before the game starts, each player can practice aiming and shooting. For this the cap is placed on the pavement with its smooth side down. Each player kneels. Holding his hand ½ inch behind the cap, he forms a trigger with his fingers, pressing the forefinger against the thumb to form an O shape. Then he snaps the forefinger forward, striking the edge of the cap.

To begin the game, a player kneels behind the outer line of the court and tries to flick his loady into box No. 13. Whoever comes closest is the first to continue. He is allowed one shot to get his loady into corner box No. 1 or on its edge. If he succeeds, he can go for box No. 2 (photograph 1). If he misses, he must wait until his next turn to try again. But his loady remains on the ground wherever it stopped, and on his next try he resumes where he left off (photograph 2). The player who was the second closest to box No. 13 on the opening shot is the next player to go.

Only one player shoots at a time, but a player can try to get an edge over an opponent. He can hit an opponent's loady out of scoring range, giving him a more difficult shot. He can also knock an opponent's loady out of a box. In either case, if he succeeds he is allowed to skip the next box ahead.

If a player accidentally knocks his own loady into the killer square, box No. 13, before he has reached box No. 12, he is deadlocked. The only way he can get back in the game is for someone to knock him out of the killer box. An opponent might do this accidentally or in an effort to skip a box. If the game is being played with partners, the partner will try to come to his rescue. Once a player reaches box No. 13, he works back through the numbers in reverse. The first to reach box No. 1 wins.

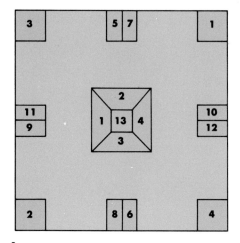

A
Figure A: One variation of skullies lasts four rounds. To begin each round, a player must shoot his loady into the numbered box at the center that corresponds to the number of the round, before continuing through the boxes on the perimeter. At the end of the fourth round, a player must shoot into box No. 13 to win.

2: The player at far right has reached box No. 4. To shoot the loady, he uses his thumb and forefinger to form a trigger. Then he flicks the loady at box No. 5.

Toys and Games
Kick-the-can

3: To free all his jailed teammates in a game of kick-the-can, a boy has come out of hiding to kick the can away from the girl who is *it*. She must return the can to its original location before she can resume her search for hidden players.

When I was young in New York, most summer days were too hot for running around. But late in the afternoon a breeze might blow off the river. Then one by one, neighborhood youngsters would climb down from their fire escapes to play a form of hide-and-seek that we called kick-the-can. The play area might include several blocks. In the middle of a game, sometimes I would sneak off for a snack before returning to my hiding spot. Today, kick-the-can is still played, but in designated and limited play areas, making capture easier and shortening the game. Even so, this game still involves the strategy and jack-rabbit quickness of a real chase.

Kick-the-can is best when it is played by five to ten youngsters. The only equipment needed is an empty soda or beer can. The play area should be limited to the length of a city block, preferably a street with many hiding places and little traffic. One place is designated the jail. This can be a bench, fire hydrant, mailbox, the space between two lampposts, or whatever.

To begin the game, the players choose *it* with the odd finger, as described under the heading, *three or more players*, in the right-hand column. The players form a circle and the one who holds the empty can throws it as far as possible. At that instant, all of the players, except *it*, run for cover. They may hide anywhere within the boundaries of the game area. *It* must retrieve the can and set it upright on the ground, returning it to the spot from where it was tossed. Then *it* must find each player and identify him by calling his name. Before *it* is allowed to capture a player, he must return to the can and tap it. Any player that *it* thus identifies must go to the jail area. Captured players remain in jail until they are rescued, which happens when a player comes out of hiding, kicks the can when *it* isn't looking, and runs back to his hiding place (as shown in photograph 3, above). This releases all players in jail, but they must hide again. Any time the can is kicked, *it* must retrieve it and return it to the starting spot before he resumes his search. Any player that *it* incorrectly identifies is permitted to kick the can and run to safety. When all the players are captured, in a game that takes place during the day, the first player to be caught becomes *it* for the next game. But when playing at night, the last boy caught becomes the new *it*. The old *it* is in charge of throwing the can as far as possible to start the game again.

Who goes first
Whatever the game, there will always be questions as to which captain gets first pick in choosing a team, which team goes first, which team will win the dispute. The ultimate solution is in the "choose."

Basic "choose" between two players
Odds and evens: One player calls odds or evens. Both close a fist and on the count of three, show one or two fingers. If they both show the same number of fingers, evens wins; if not, odds has the advantage.

Coin flip: One player calls heads or tails. A coin is tossed and the side of the coin that lands face up determines which player gets the decision.

Stickball special: One player grabs the stickball broomstick near its center. His opponent grabs the stick directly above. They alternate grips, one atop the other, until they run out of space on the stick. Whoever is gripping the top of the stick wins.

Three or more players
Odd finger is "it": Players form a circle and each closes one fist. All players call out, "One, two, three, shoot," then show either one or two fingers simultaneously. This continues until one player is caught showing a different number of fingers from all the rest and becomes "it."

Lots or straws: A strip of paper is torn into various lengths, with one piece for each player. The papers are held in a closed fist with only the tops showing. The other players draw; the one who draws the longest strip wins.

One potato, two potato: Each player sticks one foot in a circle. A caller points to one foot at a time, in sequence, for each word of this rhyme: "One potato, two potato, three potato, four; five potato, six potato, seven potato, more." The player whose foot is his target when he reaches the word "more" is chosen.

Toys and Games
Chinese handball

¢ ⊠ 👤 🏃

Chinese handball is played something like regular handball, known to city young-sters as off-the-wall ball, but it has a flavor all its own. In this game, a player must hit the ball hard against the pavement so it will bounce up, hit the wall, and land in an opponent's playing area (photograph 4).

An unobstructed wall with playing area in front of it provides the right setting. In addition, a high-bounce rubber ball is needed. The game usually includes five players. To set up the court, use sticks of chalk to mark lanes 4 to 5 feet wide on the pavement in front of the wall (Figure B). Extend these lines about 8 feet out from the base of the wall. Then, 5 feet from the wall, draw a service line across the lane on the far left.

The players draw straws to establish playing positions. The one who draws the longest straw becomes the king, the server for a game, and occupies the far left lane. Other players take the other lanes in the order determined by the length of straws drawn. The box farthest away from the king goes to the player who drew the shortest straw. Each player gets ready to defend his lane.

The king starts the game by standing at the serving line and serving the ball to any lane. To do this, he slaps the ball with an open hand against the ground so it will bounce and hit the wall. The receiver must not let the ball bounce more than once in his lane before he hits it back, bouncing it on the ground, against the wall, and into another lane. (A player is allowed to hit a ball into his own lane.) When a player misses a return, he moves to defend the lane on the far right. The other players move one box closer to the king. If the king misses a return, he loses the service and moves to the lane on the far right. Then the player closest to the left becomes the new server. A player may force an opponent to make an error by hitting a killer. A killer is a serve that strikes where the wall meets the playing surface. This makes it almost impossible for a player to return the ball. Frequently a killer shot backfires and lands in the hitter's lane. Then the error is charged against him.

In the traditional game, seven errors eliminate a player. But Chinese handball need not be played as an elimination game. Instead, it can be agreed that the player who has the fewest misses during a given number of serves becomes the king in the next game. The king must start each new service from the serving line.

Wall

Alleys

4 feet

Serving line

5 feet

8 feet

B

Figure B: For a Chinese hand ball court, mark an alley at least 4 feet wide and 8 feet long for each player in front of a playground wall with chalk. In the alley at far left draw a serving line 5 feet from the wall.

4: In Chinese handball, the server, called the king, stands at the far left and slaps the ball against the ground so it will bounce, hit the wall, and land in any other lane (drawn with chalk on the ground in front of the wall). The player guarding the lane can let the ball bounce only once, then must bounce it back and into another lane. The player who misses the return moves to the end of the line (at far right).

Toys and Games
Street stickball

5: To hit a bouncing rubber ball with a stick, wrap your fingers around the middle of its bottom half. Spread your legs, bend your knees, bend your right arm, but keep your left arm straight. Remember that you are allowed only one swing.

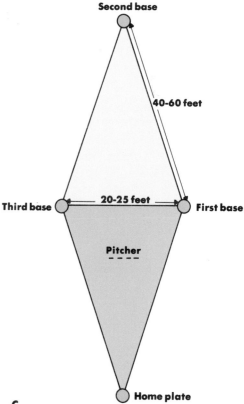

C

Figure C: A field for stickball is arranged much like a baseball diamond, except that it is narrowed and elongated to fit on a play street. If there is enough space, you can use chalk to mark bases; otherwise anything that won't blow away can be used to indicate bases and boundaries.

With no baseball diamond nearby, we used to set up a playing field in the street. All sorts of sidewalk fixtures—lampposts, mailboxes, fire hydrants—served as boundary lines. Other objects—a manhole cover, perhaps, or the door handle of a parked car—served as the bases and home plate. Baseball bats were nonexistent; we made do with a broom handle. To protect our mitt-less hands, we used a rubber ball rather than a baseball. These substitutions didn't take away a bit of the excitement of our ball game.

To play stickball, you need a stick and ball, five to seven players for each team, and ideally, a restricted play street free of traffic. With chalk or a stone, indicate the three bases, home plate and a pitching line (Figure C). Make sure that the pavement near home plate is flat; the ball must bounce once before it is swung at by the batter.

The team that bats first is determined by a *choose*, called the stickball special, page 2261. The captain of the team in the field assigns a pitcher, a catcher, and players to cover each base. If there are additional team members, they play shortstop or outfield positions. Once the batting order is established and the team in the field has warmed up, the ball can be put in play.

The pitcher starts the game by throwing overhand or underhand to the batter, but, as noted above, the ball must take one bounce before it reaches the plate. If there aren't enough players to permit a pitcher, the batter is allowed to toss the ball in the air and either hit it on the way down or after it bounces once or twice. In traditional stickball, each batter is allowed only one swing at the ball, but there is no limit to the number of balls he can let go by outside the strike area. (With younger children, three strikes and four balls are allowed, as in baseball.) A missed swing, foul ball, roofed ball, or a ball that does not come down from a fire escape is considered out. All fly balls caught put the batter out; so does a ball caught on the fly after hitting a building or a car. A fair ball that cannot be played by a fielder, as, for example, one that goes under a car, is a ground-rule double, letting the batter advance only to second base. On other hits, the batter advances from base to base as in baseball, and either crosses home plate to score or is tagged out. A team is allowed three outs in each inning, as in baseball, but a game lasts only five innings. If a car comes down the street, the first to see it yells "heads up" so the players have a chance to jump onto the sidewalk for safety.

Frank Navarra grew up in New York, playing such street games as running bases, stoop ball, box ball, and association football. He received an education degree from New York University, where he majored in recreation and camping. Frank has directed various recreational activities for the Boy's Club of New York and for Children's Village, a treatment center for emotionally disturbed children in Dobbs Ferry, New York.

Toys and Games
Running bases

Stealing bases is the most challenging part of a baseball game for many players, and that is what the game of running bases is about. A player runs between two bases that are protected by two catchers. As he runs, the catchers try to tag him out. The ability of the runner to keep his eyes on the ball at all times, to take advantage of fumbles and errors on the part of the catchers, and to race against the speeding ball determine how exciting the game becomes. When I was sixteen, in 1952, Pee Wee Reese of the Brooklyn Dodgers set a record for stealing 30 bases in one game. When we played running bases, we would try to break Reese's record.

The Shakedown

As many as ten players can participate in each inning of a game. The only equipment needed is a high-bouncing rubber ball. Use white chalk or field markers to indicate the base lines and the bases (Figure D). The running area should occupy a space approximately 10 by 60 feet. Choose to determine which members of the group will act as catchers; one stands in front of each base. The remaining players divide up into two groups. Each group lines up behind a base and gets ready to run, one at a time, when the ball is put in play. As the catchers throw the ball back and forth, the runner must race from one base to another without being tagged out. (Sometimes the game is extended by allowing each runner three outs.) The catchers may trap a runner in a rundown, as in baseball. If the runner goes outside a base line while he is being pursued he is also declared out. Any runner who intentionally blocks or interferes with the ball in play risks being called out. The two base runners who survive the longest often are awarded the positions of catchers in the next game.

Runner				Runner
Base	Catcher	Running area	Catcher	Base

D

Figure D: The square at each end of this diagram represents a safety zone for a runner in a game of running bases. Within the running lane two catchers toss a ball back and forth and guard the bases. When a runner tries to move from one safety zone to the other, the catchers try to tag him out with the ball.

Toys and Games
Kickball

A kickball field is like a baseball diamond, but the games are totally different. Instead of a bat, a kick of the foot serves to send a 10-inch rubber ball tearing across the field. There should be at least five players on each team. Chalked lines or objects such as rocks or hubcaps indicate three bases and home plate at the corners of a 45-foot square. Midway on a line between first and third base is the pitching mound.

The winners of a coin toss kick first. Members of the kicking team are given numbers to determine their kicking order. The team in the field selects a pitcher, catcher, and basemen. Any remaining players cover shortstop or the outfield. A kicker stands behind home plate, and the pitcher rolls the ball toward him. If the pitch is wild, the kicker can refuse to try to kick it. If the pitch is good, the kicker must kick the ball into the field and run as many bases as he can. If he is tagged with the ball off base, he is out. If the kick is high and caught on the fly, the kicker is out. If the ball goes out of bounds, it is a foul. If a kicker makes two fouls or misses the ball entirely with his kick, he is out. Each team is allowed three outs. There are usually seven innings to a game. The team with the most runs wins.

6: Kickball combines elements of baseball and soccer. Here, a kicker leaps high in the air in front of home plate (marked by a paper plate), after kicking a high pop-up. If it is caught on the fly he will be out; otherwise he will try to reach first base before the 10-inch ball does.

Toys and Games
Association football

7: Association football can begin with a throw-off at the center line of the playing field (above, left). This variation of football has built-in safety precautions. Rather than tackling an opponent to stop his movement, you simply tag him with both hands (above).

If you were tackled or blocked in a game of football on a city street, you would be sure to get some nasty bumps. In association football, a mild version of football in which players tag rather than tackle their opponents, the bruises are fewer but the excitement runs high as a player tries to evade the opponent at his heels.

Two to five men make up a team. The only piece of equipment needed is a football of any size. (Sometimes, we used a rolled-up newspaper about a foot long and 4 inches thick.) The play area can be a flat field, 25 by 50 yards, or a play-street area. The captains of each team choose with odd and even fingers (page 2261) to determine who will receive the ball first.

The game begins with a throw-off from the center of the field (photograph 7, top left) or a kickoff from an end zone. The receiving team attempts to advance the ball down the field by running with it or passing it. All passes—forward, backward, and lateral—are allowed at all times. After three downs (including the throw-off), the ball moves to the other team. A down occurs and play stops when the ball hits the ground, when a player holding the ball is tagged with two hands by an opponent (photograph 7, top right), or when a player runs out of bounds. After the first or second down, play is resumed with the ball going to the player who last had possession. The ball changes hands when a touchdown is scored; five touchdowns win.

Toys and Games
Hit-the-penny

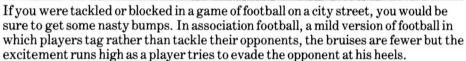

Hit-the-penny is an ideal sidewalk game because the pavement joints make an automatic game board. To play, two players center a penny or an ice-cream stick on a joint separating sidewalk squares. If a sidewalk is not available, chalk two adjacent 3-by-4-foot squares. The players stand behind the lines at opposite ends of the boxes, facing each other. Taking turns, they toss a rubber ball at the coin to hit it. The player who taps the coin receives a point. If the coin should flip over when it is hit, the player receives two points. The coin is not returned to the center line after it is hit. This happens only if the coin leaves the play area. The closer the coin moves to one end line, the more advantage the closer player has in trying to hit the coin. The first player to score 21 points wins.

Toys and Games
Hopscotch

Eight 2-foot squares drawn and numbered with chalk, as shown in the photographs, below, provide the setting for hopscotch. You also need a charm (known as a potsy in some neighborhoods) such as an ice-cream stick or crushed can lid. Any number of youngsters can participate in this game. To begin, a player stands behind the base line (the bottom edges of boxes 1 and 2). Then he gently tosses the charm into box No. 1. If the charm misses, or touches a line, the player loses his turn. If the charm lands in the box, the player must hop from boxes 2 through 8 and then back to box 2 (photograph 8, bottom left). Two feet are allowed to touch the ground at one time whenever a player lands in pairs of boxes, such as 4 and 5, or 7 and 8 (photograph below, right). Then he can put one foot on each. Back in box 2, on one foot, the player must bend over and retrieve the charm, (photograph, top left) then hop back over the base line. If the player gets this far, he repeats the entire procedure, this time tossing the charm into box 2. The player who first works his way up to box 8 and back to box 1 is the winner.

8: To make a hopscotch court, use a piece of chalk to draw 2-foot squares on the pavement like those pictured. The player tosses a lucky charm in each box in numerical order, then must hop through the boxes (right and bottom left) before retrieving the charm (below).

Toys and Games
Box ball

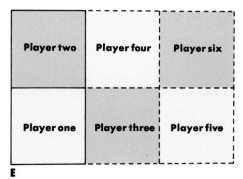

Figure E: A box-ball court can be designed for two players (solid lines) or expanded to accommodate as many as six (dotted lines). The game resembles table tennis, with players volleying a rubber ball back and forth, letting it bounce once within the box before slapping it back.

Box ball has all the slap-happiness of table tennis—but it is not played on a table. Rather, all boundary lines are drawn directly on the ground. A center line replaces the net, a rubber ball is used instead of a table-tennis ball, and hands are used as paddles. A box-ball court for two players is shown by the solid lines in Figure E. To make it, use chalk to draw two adjacent boxes, each 4 feet square. By adding more boxes as indicated by the dotted lines in Figure E, you can expand the court to accommodate as many as six players at one time, but the rules change.

With two players, each man positions himself behind the line at opposite ends of the adjoining boxes. To start a game, the players volley for service by hitting the ball back and forth, bouncing it in the opponent's box. Neither player is permitted to step over the end line while the ball is in play. During service, any ball that lands on a line is considered out; during the rest of the game it is considered in bounds. If a player misses the ball on the initial volley, hits the ball outside the perimeter of his opponent's box, or lets the ball bounce more than once before returning it, the other player wins the serve. He then must slap the ball down in his own box just in front of the end line and hit it with an underhand stroke into his opponent's box. (A server is automatically out and loses the serve if he hits the ball with a stroke other than an underhand hit.) The opponent can allow the ball to bounce only once before returning it into the server's box. The volley continues back and forth until one player makes an error, misses a ball, or slaps it out of bounds. Service change occurs if the server makes an error, the server hits the line perimeter, or the ball fails to reach the opponent's box.

The winner of the game is proclaimed king. Points are scored as follows: Each time a server causes his opponent to make an error, he receives a letter of the word, king. Only the player serving can score a letter. Although he may subsequently lose the service to his opponent, he retains any letters won for the remainder of the game. The game is over when one player gets all four letters.

All of these rules apply to the multiple-court game. In addition, once the ball is served, any player may put one foot into his own box to make it easier for him to return the ball. Any player can return a ball that was hit into a neighboring box, but if he attempts to do so, he must return the ball to the player opposite him.

Service and returned volleys can be played to any opponent's box. The server does not change in a game unless he is eliminated by winning. Then the remaining player with the most letters becomes the server. Scoring may be done in reverse; a player gets a letter for each error he makes, and when he gets all four, he is out.

Toys and Games
Stoopball or wall ball

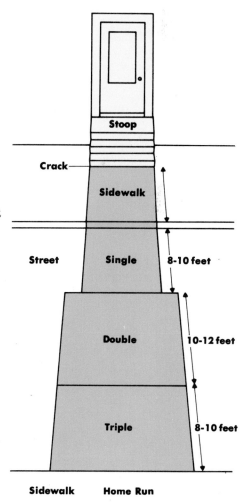

Figure F: A stoopball field is drawn so the value of the ball thrown against a stoop or wall can be determined by where it falls. One player stands on the sidewalk and tosses the ball at the point where a stoop or wall meets the sidewalk. Depending on where the ball lands, the hit is a single, double, triple, or home run.

Stoopball is a variation of baseball that eliminates the running as well as the bat. The game is played on a marked field (Figure F). To get a "hit," the player throws a rubber ball against a wall or stoop; the value of the hit is determined by which box the ball lands in. With chalk and line markers, any stoop, flat wall, or curb can be made into a playing field. The field should be divided as shown in Figure F, and should be no wider than 50 feet at its widest point. Each team should have an even number of players, with as many as six men to a side. A toss of a coin will determine which team gets to throw first. Fielders of the opposing team should position themselves anywhere behind the infield line.

A player can throw the ball into the crack at the base of the stoop to make it travel farther. By the rules, however, the ball must not hit the sidewalk before or after it hits the stoop, or the pitcher is out. The value of the hit is determined by the marked area in which the ball first falls. No bases are run. Foul balls or balls caught on the fly are out. Although the game moves faster if each man gets only one pitch, you might want to let each man continue pitching until he is put out. Each team is allowed three outs, and the game lasts five or seven innings.

Toys and Games
Follow-the-leader

With a good-humored leader, a playground with swings, climbing bars, oversized pipes, and statues can be turned into a maze for a rousing game of follow-the-leader, such as the one pictured (photograph 9).

Any number of youngsters can play. The leader needn't be a good athlete, but he should be able to dream up tasks both easy and difficult.

To begin, the players line up behind the leader, with at least an arm's length between them. Then the leader digs into his bag of tricks to fool the followers. He may whimsically head in any direction, using any waddle, hop, skip, or jump that he chooses. Any player unable to keep up with his antics is eliminated. The player who follows until he is the only follower left becomes the leader of the next game. To avoid eliminating players, you can send followers who can't keep up with the leader to the end of the line.

Toys and Games
Ring-a-levio

Ring-a-levio is a fast action game of hide-and-seek. The playing field should be bounded on each end by a marker such as a lamppost or bench. Designate one end of the field as the jail. To begin, two captains are selected. They should choose evenly matched teams to keep the game from continuing indefinitely. The captains determine which team is to hide first. As the running team counts to 50, players on the other team can hide anywhere within bounds. One member of the running team acts as a jail guard while runners search for the enemy. If a runner catches an enemy, he must hold him long enough to say, "Ring-a-levio 1, 2, 3," three times (photograph 10). Then the prisoner must go to jail. But all of the prisoners escape if a free teammate runs through the jail. Or, if there are enough prisoners to make a human chain, they may be able to grab an unsuspecting jail guard and pull him into the jail. Then the prisoners can run and hide again. It takes good teamwork to find and catch the fastest and most agile of the players. When all of the hiders are jailed, the other team hides and the game begins all over again.

9: These boys and girls are busy keeping up with the stunts of the boy in blue as they climb over playground sculptures in a challenging game of follow-the-leader.

10: The playground umbrella in the background serves as the jail for a game of hide-and-seek called ring-a-levio. By the time the running team counts to 50, all of the other players must hide. Any tagged runner must stay in jail until he is freed by a teammate or is able to pull a prison guard into the jail.

Toys and Games
Double dutch

¢ ☒ ⚲

Jump rope is an age-old schoolyard game. Over the years, a complex version has developed called double dutch. This game involves two ropes of the same length, swung simultaneously in opposite directions while one girl jumps them both. As pictured below, one rope sweeps under the jumper's feet while the other swings over her head. To keep from stumbling, the jumper must move in double time.

In double dutch, the ropes should be 8 feet long. Each rope twirler holds one rope end in her right hand and the other in her left. The rope in the right hand is swung toward the right and the other toward the left. The key to a good game is in the timing of the twirlers and the jumper. The twirlers swing the rope evenly with a moderate tempo. If the rope moves too slowly, it will be impossible for the jumper to keep up a steady tempo, and if it is swung too fast—called hot pepper—it will be hard for the jumper to keep up with the pace.

The jumper stands beside the ropes as they turn, sways to their rhythm, and jumps in when she can. As one rope ascends she quickly skips over the bottom rope. To keep from losing her turn, the jumper must continue to skip over any rope that swings toward her ankles.

By keeping track of how many times she repeats a rhyme, the jumper can gauge how well she has done. Sometimes a twirler keeps score. For every ten turns of the rope, the twirler awards one point to the jumper. After each jumper has had a turn, whoever has the most points is designated the winner. Losers take turns twirling the rope, so everyone gets a chance to jump.

Jingles or nonsense rhymes are often sung by all players in a rhythmic chant as a jumper skips through the air. Among them are:

Fudge, fudge, call the judge.
Mama's got a newborn babe.
Wrap it up in tissue paper.
Send it up the elevator.
First floor, stop. (Jumper stops.)
Second floor, miss. (Jumper misses.)
Third floor, turn around. (Jumper turns around.)
Fourth floor, touch the ground.
(Jumper touches ground.)
Fifth floor, get out of town. (Jumper jumps out.)

Red, hot, pepper, with the H, O, T!
Ten, twenty, thirty, forty, fifty (and so on, rope turning faster and faster until the jumper misses).

Teddy bear, teddy bear, turn around,
Teddy bear, teddy bear, touch the ground,
Teddy bear, teddy bear, touch your toe,
Teddy bear, teddy bear, touch your shoe,
Teddy bear, teddy bear, now skidoo.

2-4-6-8-
Meet me at the garden gate,
If I'm late, please don't wait,
2-4-6-8.

Fire, fire false alarm,
I fell into (name)'s arms

11: In double-dutch jump rope, one rope swings over the jumper's head as the other passes beneath her feet. Some rhymes that give rhythm to this game are at right, above.

STRING ART
Curves From Straight Lines

Richard Ohanian, an architectural student at Ohio State University, considers his string art to be intimately related to architecture. He also creates environmental sculptures and outdoor graphic designs. His work has been exhibited in many shows and is represented in collections in Ohio, Pennsylvania, Indiana, Texas, and New York.

Curves made up of straight lines? Such is the case in geometric string art. A finished piece might seem to contain a multitude of curves, but in fact there will not be a single one. All of the curves are made of tiny straight-line segments. The human eye is just not sensitive enough to see them as anything but curves.

String art is believed to have originated in 1906 in a kingergarten teacher's manual, written by an Englishwoman, Edith Somervell. Her *Rhythmic Approach to Mathematics* is a teaching aid for mathematics study. The preface, by Mary Everest Boole, reports that in 1898, these two women acquired drawings of curves made of straight lines from a man named Benjamin Betts, who had retired to a Brazilian forest to study philosophy. Mrs. Somervell saw in his drawings a link between "an organic thought sequence and the evolution of form." The example she used, called the curve of pursuit, is illustrated at left. The curve is created by the interaction of a rabbit and a hungry dog. As the rabbit runs toward the safety of the burrow, the dog changes course to follow him. The straight lines represent the dog's wishes—to get to the rabbit when the rabbit is at some particular point. The curve represents the dog's actions when the rabbit continues to move. Hence the name, the curve of pursuit. Whether or not you find philosophy in string art, the pieces are intriguing and quite simple to construct.

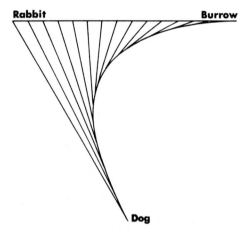

The straight lines represent the dog's line of sight; the curve represents his actions as the rabbit moves toward the burrow. Called the curve of pursuit, this was one of the first examples of how to create a curve with straight lines. It was included in a teacher's manual written by Edith Somervell in 1906.

Materials

In flat compositions, the backboard is standard ½-inch plywood, cut to whatever geometric shape will best display the composition. Plywood is strong enough to absorb the tremendous pull of the threads, securely holding the nails. The type of nails used depends on the design to be strung. For a simple, straight-sided geometric, 19-gauge brads ½-inch long are adequate. For a design that requires that more than a few threads be wrapped around each nail, use ⅝-inch nails with flat heads that will keep the threads from slipping off. The fabric used to cover the plywood and the thread used for stringing depend on the visual effect sought. The overlapping layers of these designs should not need to compete with a vivid background color. Try to keep the color scheme bright but not wild. The best fabrics for covering the board will, when stretched, lie smoothly but have a finely textured appearance. Wool flannel, corduroy, velvet, and polyester crepe work well. Among the stringing materials are nylon thread, copper wire, and wool knitting-yarn; each has advantages. But the one I find most satisfactory is mercerized cotton-wrapped polyester thread. It is available in a wide variety of colors, it can be overlapped indefinitely, it remains elastic in humid or dry weather, and it keeps a constant tension so the curve remains true. To facilitate handling the thread, make a threadholder by driving a nail into a scrap of wood. Place the spool of thread on the nail; the thread will unwind easily while the spool stays in place.

You will also need: a saw for cutting and sandpaper for smoothing the plywood; scissors to cut the fabric; a steam iron to press it; and a staple gun to attach it. And you need a long straightedge, triangle, compass, protractor, pencil, eraser, and paper for making the pattern; and a hammer, screw eyes, and wire to hang the completed work.

This string composition, made of clear sheet acrylic and white sewing thread, is mounted on a plywood stand with a built-in light source. Instructions for making this design begin on page 2280.

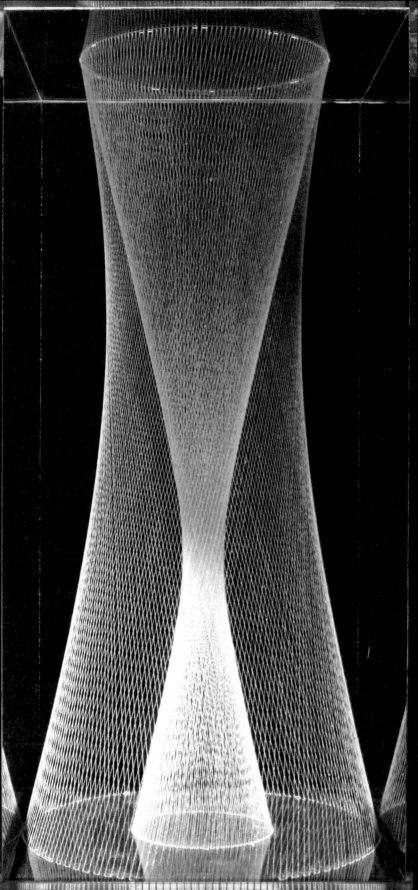

1: To cover a piece of plywood with fabric, staple one edge of the fabric to the board, pull the fabric tight, and staple the opposite edge, working from the center toward the corners. The same technique can be used for geometric shapes other than a rectangle, as long as there are an even number of sides.

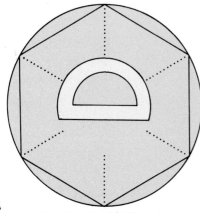

A
Figure A: To make a six-sided shape from a circle, place a protractor on a circle's diameter and mark segments of 60 degrees. Extend these marks through the center to the perimeter of the circle; then connect the outer intersections to form a hexagon.

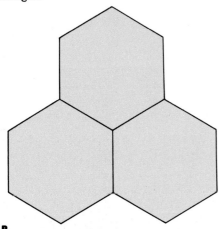

B
Figure B: After drawing and cutting out three hexagons of the same size, place them side by side to form the pattern shape shown.

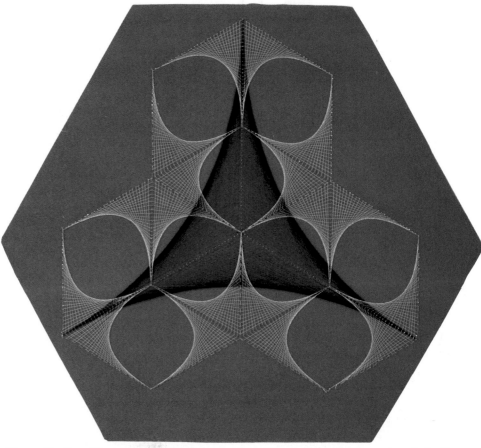

The combination of three hexagons placed side by side on a blue hexagonal background results in this unusual design. The triangular layer of thread, worked in black, connects the outer points of the three hexagons. The white top layer is worked within the sides of each hexagon.

Graphic Arts
Three adjacent hexagons $ ▧ ♟ ✈

The string composition pictured above is based on one geometric shape, the hexagon. By connecting three hexagons, a new shape is created. The string design is then worked inside this geometric framework. In this design the first layer, worked in black thread, connects the outer points of the three hexagons. The second layer, in white thread, is worked in six angles within each hexagon.

The Backboard
To make the backboard, you need a piece of plywood at least 3 inches longer and wider than your design, plus sandpaper, a piece of fabric 6 inches larger and wider than the plywood, and a staple gun. You can leave the plywood square or cut it into the shape pictured. (Note that the sides are not of equal lengths—three sides are 15 inches long and three are 18 inches.) Sand the edges and corners and dust the board. Place the fabric right side down and put the plywood, smoother side down, on top of it. Staple along one edge of the fabric. Pull the opposite edge of the fabric so it will be smooth across the front of the board and staple it, starting in the center and working out to the corners (photograph 1). Continue pulling the fabric taut as you staple. Repeat with opposite edges until they are all stapled down. Fold the fabric at the corners and secure it with several staples.

The Pattern
To make a hexagon pattern, start by drawing a circle approximately the size you want each hexagon to be. In the design pictured, the circle has a diameter of 14 inches. Place a protractor on the diameter of the circle, and mark off segments of 60

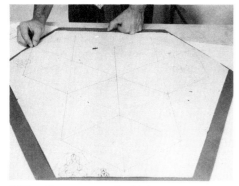

2: Place the pattern on the fabric-covered board, centering the design on the board. To hold the pattern, drive a nail in the center of the design and at each of the outer corners.

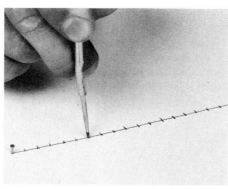

3: Using the pointed end of a compass, make a hole through the pattern, fabric, and into the plywood at ¼-inch intervals along all of the pattern lines (Figure C).

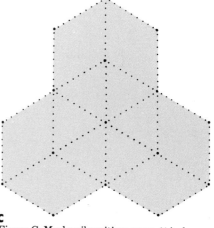

C

Figure C: Mark nail positions every ¼ inch around the shape and along the inner lines.

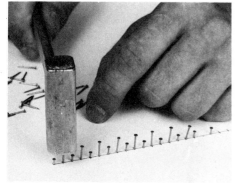

4: Put a nail in every other pattern hole and drive it in. Then put nails in the holes left blank and hammer them in. This procedure helps keep the line perfectly straight.

5: When all of the nails needed for the string design are in place, rip the pattern off the board with one steady pull, so it comes off in one piece. Hammer in any loose nails.

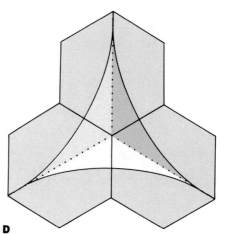

D

Figure D: The first layer has three large curves that join the outer points of the three adjacent hexagons. These curves are made from the broad angles formed by the three hexagon diameters which meet in the center of the composition.

degrees (Figure A). Through each of these marks, draw lines connecting the center of the circle with the outside of the circle. Connect the perimeter points with straight lines; the result is a hexagon (a figure with six equal sides). Make two more identical hexagon patterns the same way; cut out all three. Place them on a piece of paper so they are touching as shown in Figure B. Trace them to obtain the final pattern. As a guide for driving the ½-inch brads, connect the outer corner of each hexagon with the opposite inner corner, and mark off ¼-inch segments along the lines (Figure C). Also, mark segments around the perimeter of the shape. Place the pattern on the fabric-covered plywood where you want the design to be. Put a nail in the design center and in each outer corner—to hold the pattern (photograph 2). Then, using the point of a compass, punch a hole through the pattern and fabric and into the plywood at each ¼-inch mark (photograph 3). Drive a nail in every other hole. Then insert and drive nails in the holes between (photograph 4). This is easier than trying to drive a nail every ¼ inch. With all the nails in place, rip the pattern off the board (photograph 5). Straighten any nails that are not in line.

Layers of String

The bottom layer of string, worked in black, is made of three large curves across the hexagons (Figure D). The nails for these curves run from the center of the pattern to the outer corner of each hexagon. Since one line of nails is used in two adjacent curves, the three lines of nails serve to make three long curves. String these curves by following the directions for making curves with a double loop (Craftnotes, page 2275).

The top layer of string, worked in white, is made with 18 small curves, six inside each hexagon. Use the nails indicated in Figure E, and string these curves by using a single loop (Craftnotes, page 2275). To hang your completed string art, put two screw eyes, with wire between them, in the back of the plywood.

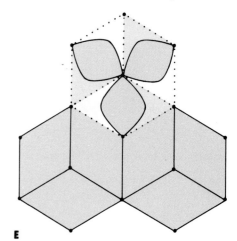

E

Figure E: A second (white string) layer of six curves is formed within each hexagon, joining three outer points with the center. Each curve uses the angle formed by the perimeter and one of the lines that divide the hexagon into thirds. The six curves form three petal shapes.

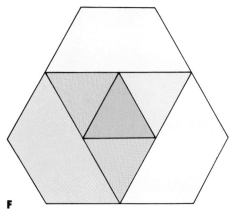

F

Figure F: To make a pattern for the irregular six-sided shape shown in the photograph at right, overlap half of three hexagons.

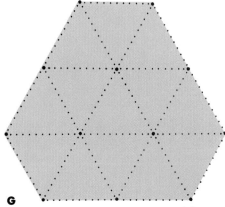

G

Figure G: Put nails every ¼ inch around the perimeter of the shape and along intersecting lines that connect opposite corners, so a triangle is formed in the middle.

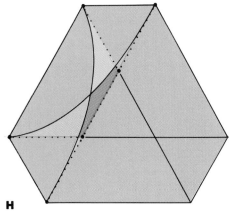

H

Figure H: The first layer of string has six curves, two strung on the outside of each intersecting line. One overlapping pair of these six curves is shown above. The angle on which each is strung is twice as tall as it is wide.

The three hexagons used in the project pictured on page 2272 are simply overlapped (Figure F) to create this shape, which has three long sides and three short sides. String is threaded in three layers, the dark brown first, then rust, then light yellow on top.

Graphic Arts

Triple stellate forms

$ ⊠ 🚶 ✈

The string curve possesses two characteristics that contribute to its design value: translucency and continuity. The translucency of the curve allows one to overlap various curves many times. With each different layer, smaller and denser shapes result in colors ranging from dark to light. The continuity of curves gives rise to the formation of larger shapes; the end of one curve can become the beginning of the next. Areas not filled with string become as important to the design as the string areas. A controlled color scheme, relatively monochromatic in the design shown above, lets layers combine visually with each other.

This design starts with the same three hexagons used in the previous project, but rather than being placed adjacent to each other, they overlap (Figure F). This results in a shape with three long sides and three short sides. Make the pattern with three hexagons; then trace around the shape. Draw intersecting lines connecting opposite corners and forming a triangle in the center (Figure G). The ½-inch brads will go along these lines and around the perimeter of the shape. Mark the lines into ¼-inch segments. Cut and cover the backboard, following the directions on page 2272. Place the pattern on top of the backboard and drive brads at the corners and the points of the center triangle to hold the pattern in place. Then hammer in a brad at each ¼-inch mark, and pull the pattern off the board. Make sure the brads form straight lines.

Three Colors of Thread

To string this design, you will need thread in each of three colors. The first layer, worked in dark brown in the design shown above, is made of six one-to-two ratio

CRAFTNOTES: MAKING STRING-ART CURVES

The single loop: Knot the thread on the top nail in the vertical row of the figure you are starting. Take the thread under the inside horizontal nail and loop it around the second horizontal nail, as shown above.

Take the thread over the second vertical nail and loop it around the third, as shown above; then take the thread down to the next horizontal nail. Continue stringing this way. The result will be a single loop of thread on each nail and a single strand of thread between pairs of nails.

The double loop: Knot the thread on the top nail in the vertical row. Take the thread down and around the inside horizontal nail, as shown above.

Take the thread around the second vertical nail, then around the second horizontal nail, as shown above. Continue stringing this way until all nails have been wrapped. The result will be two strands of thread between each pair of nails.

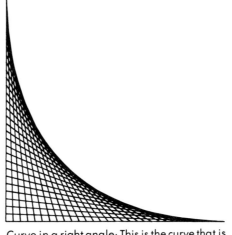

Curve in a right angle: This is the curve that is formed when you string rows of nails that form a right angle.

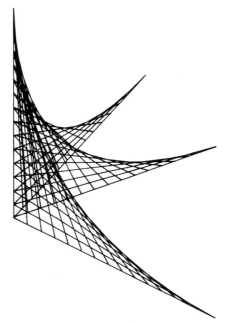

Curves in acute or obtuse angles: Curves that are wide or narrow are formed in angles that are wide or narrow. The wider the angle of nails, the flatter the curve will be; the narrower the angle, the deeper the curve, as shown in the curve variations above.

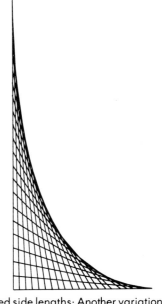

Varied side lengths: Another variation in the curve results if one of its sides is twice as long as the other. To construct this curve, place the nails in one row every ¼ inch, the nails in the other row ½ inch apart (or use every other nail). This gives you a one-to-two ratio curve. Other ratios are possible, such as two-to-three or one-to-three.

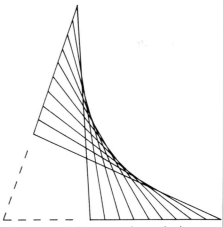

An open-ended curve can be worked on a portion of two lines of nails that form an angle, rather than on the entire line, to form unusual shapes.

curves, using the double-loop method of stringing (see Craftnotes above). These curves have one side twice as long as the other. Use every other brad on the long side and every brad on the short side. Two curves are strung on each of these intersecting lines (Figure H). The top two-thirds, then the bottom two-thirds of the line make the longer sides of the curves so they overlap in the center third.

In the second layer, worked in rust-colored thread, are three regular curves that use the same nails as the first layer (Figure I, page 2276). But these curves overlap in the center triangle and are strung using the double-loop method (see Craftnotes above). The light yellow top layer, also done with the double-loop method, looks

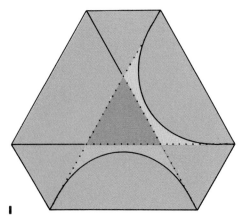

I

Figure I: The second layer of string in the composition on page 2274 has three curves. Their angles overlap in the center triangle. Two of the three curves are shown above.

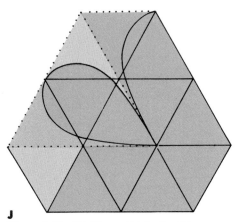

J

Figure J: The third layer of string has 12 curves. Pairs of them are strung into each of the six corners of the shape; facing curves create teardrop shapes. Three of these curves are shown above.

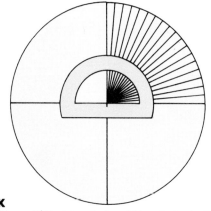

K

Figure K: To string circles within a circle, start by drawing the outer circle and two diameters at right angles. Place a protractor on one diameter, and mark off every 5 degrees. Draw lines from the center of the circle through these marks to the perimeter of the circle.

more complicated than it is. It is made of twelve one-to-two ratio curves in clusters of two at each of the six outer corners of the three hexagon shapes (Figure J). Two-thirds of each intersecting line form the long side of the angle, while the short side lies along the perimeter of the design, either along a short side or along half of a long side. Two adjacent curves along a long side form a teardrop shape. When this layer is complete, there are three such teardrops, with pointed ends overlapping in the center. To hang the completed composition, put two screw eyes into the back of the plywood and attach a hanging wire.

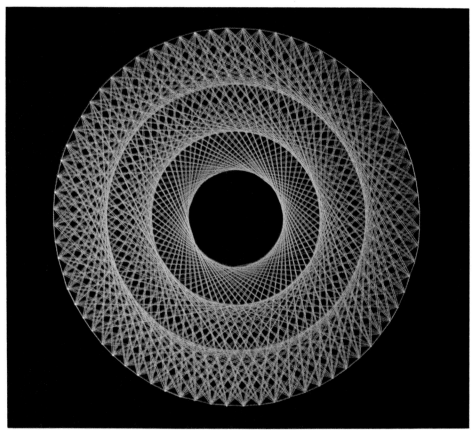

This straightforward design of concentric circles has a dramatic look when it is created with a gold-colored cotton thread displayed against a background of black velvet.

Graphic Arts

Helios

$ 🔲 🧍 🛩

In the previous string-art projects, brads were driven in straight lines, thread was strung in straight lines, and the design was curved. But in the project shown above, the brads are driven in a circle, the thread is strung in straight lines, and the design that results has circles within circles. The stringing methods are the same as those used in angles. You can use the double-loop procedure (Craftnotes, page 2275), going from one brad to another, back to the first, then to the brad next to the second. Or you can use the single-loop method going from one brad to another, then around its adjacent brad before you go back across the circle.

To make a pattern for this design, draw a circle with a compass or a string tied to a pencil. The circle pictured is 16 inches in diameter. Draw two diameter lines across the circle at right angles. Place a protractor on one diameter and mark every 5 degrees. Then connect these points with the center of the circle (Figure K). Extend these lines to the circumference of the circle to get the nail points. There will be 72 marks on the circle. Place this pattern on a fabric-covered board, either centered or off-center depending on your preference. Use the point of the compass to make starting holes for the brads. Drive the brads through the pattern into the backboard at each mark; then pull the pattern from the board. This design has concentric circles that seem to radiate from the open center, each circle growing larger. They are formed by straight threads from one point to another on the circle's perimeter. The shorter the distance between nails, the larger the circle formed. The design shown above is dramatic because a bold color scheme was used; the backboard is covered with black velvet and the design is worked in gold-colored (not metallic) thread. To start stringing, tie the thread to a brad at the bottom of the circle. The first circle is started by connecting the first and the 30th brad, counting to the right (Figure L). Once you count 30 brads and connect this thread, take the thread back to the next brad on the right of the bottom brad; then back up to the brad on the left of the 30th brad so you do not have to count 30 brads each time. As you proceed around the perimeter, you will form a small circle in the center. The second layer of thread is started by connecting the first and the 25th brad (Figure M). As you proceed you will form a circle slightly larger than the first circle. The top layer is started by connecting the first and the 18th brad (Figure N). When you finish stringing, knot the thread around the last brad and cut off any excess.

For a different effect, you could string each layer of thread with a different color, or you could change the size of the circles as did the children pictured on page 2283. When you have completed the composition, put two screw eyes in the back of the plywood and attach a hanging wire to them.

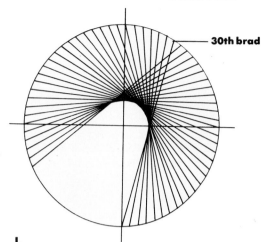

L

Figure L: To start the first layer of thread, connect the bottom brad with one 30 brads to the right; then move to the right of the first brad and to the left of the 30th. This will create a small circle in the center.

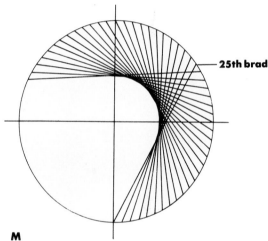

M

Figure M: Start the second layer of thread by connecting the bottom brad with one 25 brads to the right. As you advance the stringing you will create a larger circle in the center.

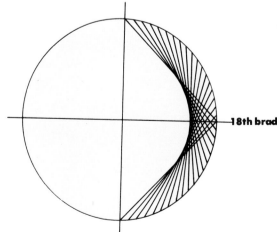

N

Figure N: In the third layer of thread connect the bottom brad with one 18 brads to the right to start the largest circle of the three layers.

String art can be designed to fit a specific room by selecting appropriate colors and by choosing shapes that complement the furnishings in the room.

This close-up of the oval at right shows that each layer of thread is strung ⅛ inch higher than the previous layer, so the ten layers just reach the top of the nails.

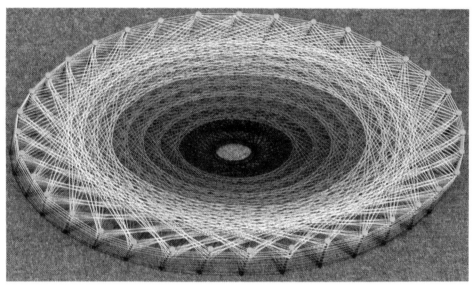

To create a three-dimensional look with two-dimensional threading techniques, each of the ten layers of thread is looped slightly higher on nails that project 1¼ inches above the background.

Graphic Arts
Raised ellipse

The ellipse design pictured above has a three-dimensional look but is made with a two-dimensional technique of stringing. Long nails are used, so each of the several layers of thread can be raised until the top layer is at the top of the nails. The result is the formation of a bowl in the middle of the ellipse. You can use ½-inch plywood for the backboard, but use No. 10 common nails, about 1¾ inches long. You will need 36 nails.

To make the pattern for the ellipse, decide on the dimensions you want the ellipse to be. The one pictured is 10 by 18 inches. Start with two concentric circles, one the diameter of the smaller dimension of the ellipse, the other the diameter of the larger dimension of the ellipse (Figure O). With a protractor, mark every 10 degrees and extend these lines through both circles. Where these lines cross the smaller circle, draw horizontal lines outside the small circle. Where these lines cross the larger circle, draw vertical lines in toward the center. These horizontal and vertical lines will meet at points along the perimeter of the ellipse. Connect these points to get the ellipse shape; use the degree lines as marks for the nails.

Drive the nails through the fabric-covered plywood so the points break the back surface. Then turn the board over and tap the nail points back until they are flush with the back surface (photograph 6), thus making all nails the same height.

The bowl-shaped ellipse pictured is made of ten layers of thread in five shades, ranging from pale gray to a deep charcoal gray. To duplicate this, you will need only one spool of each shade. The ellipse is strung the same way as a circle using the double-loop method (Craftnotes, page 2275). Start the first layer of the ellipse by connecting the first nail and the 17th nail; these threads will form a small ellipse in the center. Push the first layer of thread down flush with the fabric. For the second layer, connect the first and the 16th nail; for the third layer, connect the first and the 15th nail. Continue this way, moving one nail closer to the starting nail for each successive layer until you have ten layers.

Place each of the successive layers ⅛ inch above the previous layer. Cut a strip of paper or tape to the desired height, and wrap it around the outside of the nails before stringing that layer. Work the stringing at the top of the nails (photograph 7); then push the thread down to the top of the paper strip (photograph 8). The ten layers should be evenly spaced along the height of the nail (photograph 9).

This string art design can be displayed horizontally on a tabletop like a piece of sculpture. It could also be hung on a wall.

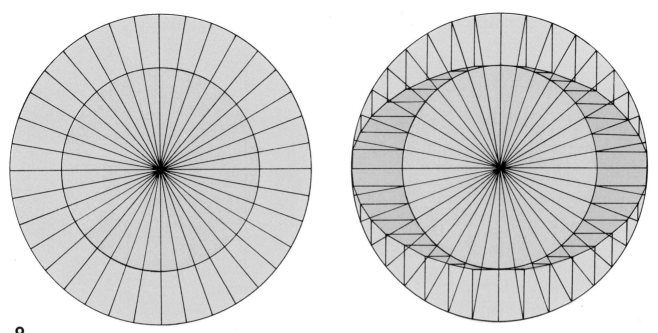

O

Figure O: To make an ellipse—a flattened circle—draw two concentric circles with diameters equal to the width and length of the desired ellipse. Use a protractor along the length to mark every 10 degrees; extend these lines through both circles (left). Where these lines cross the smaller circle, draw horizontal lines outside the small circle. Where these same lines touch the larger circle, draw vertical lines back toward the center line. Connect the points where horizontal and vertical lines meet to get the outline of the ellipse (right).

6: To make sure the nails will be the same height, drive the nails through the plywood until the points break the back surface; then tap the nail points back until they are flush with the board.

7: As a stringing guide, cut a strip of paper to the height you want, and wrap it around the base of the nails. Then string that layer of thread on the nails anywhere above the paper strip.

8: When that layer of thread is complete and you have knotted the end of it to the nail, push the entire layer down until it touches the top of the paper strip.

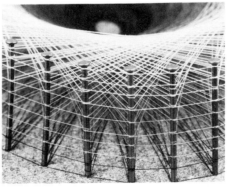

9: For the best design effect, the ten layers of thread should be evenly spaced along the height of each nail. If you use a different number of layers, adjust the spacing accordingly.

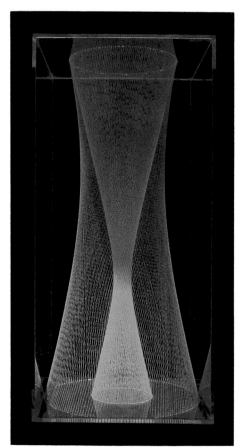

By changing the light bulb from white (page 2271) to blue, you can change the mood created by this three-dimensional string-art design.

Graphic Arts
Conics in a box

The ethereal string sculpture pictured at left and on page 2271 was created by working in three dimensions within a box of acrylic plastic, then lighting the composition from below. The effect is that of a geometric form floating in space.

To make such a sculpture—the one pictured is a column 2 feet tall and 1 foot square—you will need: six pieces of ¼-inch clear sheet acrylic, two that are 12 inches square, two that are 12 by 23½ inches, and two that are 11½ by 23½ inches; the acrylic solvent that is used to glue this material; one spool of white thread; and a tapestry needle. Places that sell sheet acrylic are listed under "Plastics" in the Yellow Pages. In many cases you can have the acrylic cut to size for a small fee. Sand the edges with a fine grade of wet-or-dry sandpaper until they are smooth. The acrylic comes with layers of protective paper covering both sides to prevent scratches; do not remove this until you finish work on that piece. To make holes in the acrylic, you will need an electric drill.

Drawing the Pattern
On the paper covering of the bottom 12-inch square, draw two concentric circles, one 4½ inches in diameter, the other 11½ inches in diameter. Using a protractor, mark off 5-degree segments, extending lines through these points from the center to the perimeter of the outer circle (photograph 10). On the other 12-inch square, which will be the top of the cube, draw one 8-inch circle and mark off 5-degree segments. Use the electric drill to make holes where the lines intersect, on all three circles (photograph 11). Keep the drill as perpendicular as you can, so the holes will be vertical. When all the holes are drilled, remove the paper covering from both sides of the 12-inch squares and from one side only (the inside surface) of the two 12-by-23½-inch pieces. You will assemble these pieces in an open-sided box so the long pieces rest on the bottom square and the top square rests on the long pieces, making the total height 24 inches. Glue these pieces together with acrylic solvent, following the manufacturer's instructions (photograph 12).

Stringing
To speed stringing, work sections of 15 to 20 holes at one time with a 12-foot-long thread and a tapestry needle. To make the knot that begins or ends a segment, tie an end of the thread over itself many times. Then pull the knot until it is hidden in the thickness of the acrylic (Figure P). If the knot pulls through the hole, it is not large enough. Take the thread from the starting hole in the top circle diagonally to a point 5 or 10 holes to one side of the hole directly opposite in the small circle. The more you slant the thread, the smaller will be the circle formed in the center; if you angle the thread straight across the circle, all the threads will cross at the center point (Figure Q). If you do not angle the thread at all, you will form a cylinder if the circles are the same size; a megaphone-shape if the circles are of different sizes.

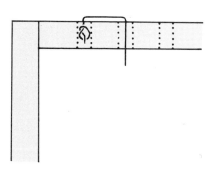

P

Figure P: To start a thread, make a knot by tying the end of the thread over itself several times. Then pull the knot until it is lodged snugly in one of the holes in the ¼-inch acrylic.

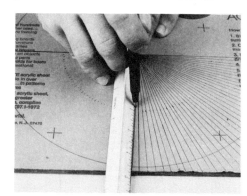

10: To locate the holes you will drill, draw a circle on the paper covering and mark off every 5 degrees with a protractor. Extend lines from the center through the marks to the perimeter.

11: With an electric drill, drill holes where the 5-degree lines intersect the perimeter of the circle, going all the way through the ¼-inch sheet of acrylic. Keep the drill perpendicular.

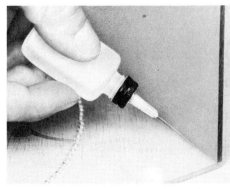

12: To glue two pieces of sheet acrylic together at a right angle, use acrylic solvent and follow the manufacturer's directions. Here, a side piece of the cube is being glued to the top piece.

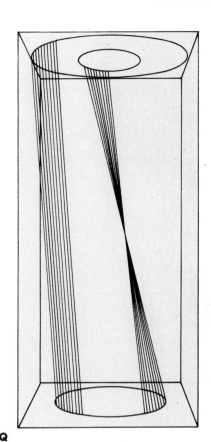

Q

Figure Q: If you string the thread from one circle to the same point on the perimeter of a larger or smaller circle opposite, you will form a megaphone shape. But if you take the thread down on a diagonal line, you will form a megaphone shape with a twist.

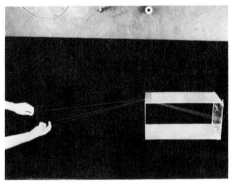

13: Take the thread from a small circle at one end to the single larger circle at the other end, then back again. Continue threading this way, pulling the thread taut each time you have threaded three pairs of holes.

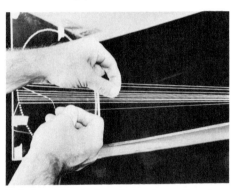

14: Before tying the knot that ends a section of thread, pull on the first thread in that section and on each subsequent thread in order until all the threads are taut, but don't pull so hard that the thread breaks.

Experiment with stringing until you achieve an effect you like. Outside the box, take the thread to the adjacent hole in the small circle, then back up to the adjacent hole in the top circle. Continue threading this way, pulling the thread tight every three holes (photograph 13). If you thread more holes before tightening the thread, it might tangle. Before tying the knot that ends the section, pull on the first thread, then on each successive thread in order, to make sure all threads are taut but not stretched so much they might break (photograph 14). Continue stringing the inner cones in this manner until they are finished. Then string the outer cone the same way, taking the thread diagonally from the top circle to a point on the larger bottom circle and back to the top circle.

To finish the acrylic cube, remove the protective paper from the outside of the open-sided box and from both sides of the two remaining long pieces of acrylic. Using dull table knives like shoehorns, slide the remaining two sides into place, and cement them there with acrylic solvent.

Displaying the String Sculpture

This design can be made to look like a fiber optic—a sculpture created with thread-like filaments of light. Place the design on a stand that has a light source inside (Figure R). The stand I made is 12 inches square so the acrylic cube fits neatly on it. It could be 1 foot tall for displaying the design on a mantel or shelf, but I wanted the stand to sit on the floor so I made it 3½ feet tall. I used four pieces of ½-inch plywood, two 3½ feet tall by 11 inches wide and two 3½ feet tall by 12 inches wide, held together with scraps of wood glued at the top and bottom corners. The pedestal has neither a top nor a bottom, of course, but several holes should be drilled in the sides near the floor edge so heat from the light bulb can dissipate. A 60-watt bulb in a porcelain socket provides the light.

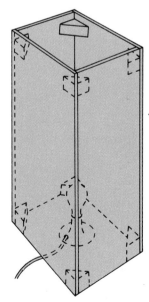

R

Figure R: The sculpture stand is made of four pieces of ½-inch-thick plywood, held together with glue and reinforced with blocks at the corners. A light bulb in a porcelain socket sitting on the floor illuminates the string art. Drill several holes near the bottom of the open-ended plywood box for ventilation.

Rae Hoff has been teaching art in East Rockaway, New York, to elementary and junior high school students for many years. She has a bachelor's degree in art education from New York University and a master's degree from the Waldorf Institute at Adelphi University; she studied string art while she was earning that degree. Rae has taught student teachers from Hofstra and Adelphi Universities, Long Island, New York, and has been active in art workshops.

Children's designs

"When we started this, I thought you were teaching us math; I didn't think it was going to be so beautiful," said one ten-year-old child who had just learned to create a string art design. She was enthusiastic about the designs, but at the same time, she was learning geometric shapes and their relation to one another.

The eight-year-olds, the youngest children in the group, learned they could make curves by stringing two straight lines. They used paper plates, pencils, ruler, T pins, No. 5 pearl cotton embroidery thread in various colors, an embroidery needle, and cellophane tape. The child draws an angle (or several angles) on the paper plate with pencil and ruler, then marks off ¼-inch intervals along both lines of the angle (photograph 15). Using a T pin, he makes a hole at each of the ¼-inch marks (photograph 16). Provided with a threaded needle, he brings the needle up from the back at the end mark of one of the angle lines, not the corner (Figure S). He pulls the thread until there is only a short tail left on the back and tapes this to the plate. Figure S shows how to start the stringing. He continues connecting holes (rather than looping nails). When he runs out of thread, he tapes the tail to the back of the paper-plate and starts the next length of thread at the next hole. Completed paper-plate designs made by children are shown at left.

Nine-year-olds used a cardboard circle as a pattern to make circular string-art designs on plywood. Each one sanded the plywood and covered it with fabric or velour paper. Using 1-inch-long, 17-gauge wire nails and a light hammer and following the edge of the cardboard circle, the child put nails in the plywood (photograph 17). Then he strung a circular design as shown on page 2277, using a different color thread for each layer (photograph 18). The children's circles are pictured opposite, bottom.

Ten-year-olds learned to make a hexagon from a circle using a compass (Figure T). They used heavy cardboard, made holes in it with a T pin, and strung the design with a needle and thread. Their designs are shown opposite, top. They could also cover a piece of plywood, and hammer nails into it to hold a design.

Stringing angles—obtuse and acute as well as right angles—drawn on a paper plate to make brightly colored curves provide an introduction to string art design.

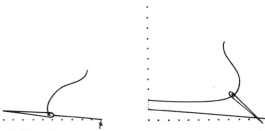

15: To start, draw any angle on a paper plate, using a ruler and pencil. Mark off ¼-inch intervals on the lines.

16: Using a T pin, make a hole through the paper plate at each of the ¼-inch marks. Make sure each line has the same number of marks.

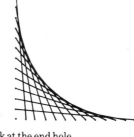

S

Figure S: To string the angle, start by bringing the thread up from the back at the end hole on one end of the lines (not at the corner). Tape the end to the back of the plate. Take the thread to the hole nearest the corner on the other line, then back up to the hole next to it. Take the thread across the angle to the second hole in the bottom line. Continue this way until all the holes are used.

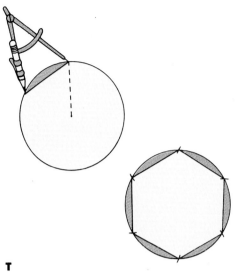

Using the techniques of stringing angles and circles, these children drew geometric figures and filled them in individual ways to form these striking designs.

T
Figure T: To start with a circle and make a hexagon from a circle, set the compass to the length of the radius of the circle, then use it to make segments around the perimeter of the circle. When these six marks are joined with straight lines, a hexagon is formed (right).

17: A cardboard circle is used as a guide as nails are driven to make a circular pattern on fabric-covered plywood.

Each of these children started with a circle of nails driven into fabric-covered plywood and each produced a different design, depending on the size of the circles and the color of the thread used.

18: A circular design can then be strung (page 2277). Several layers of string are used.

STRUCTURAL FURNISHINGS
Looking Up for Living Space

A homeowner, pressed for ways to better use his house, tends to think horizontally. How can a given floor space be cut into more cubicles to provide, say, an extra bedroom, an additional closet, or a new den? The result, all too often: boxes within boxes and more crowding of already cramped living space.

There is often an alternative. Many home craftsmen are raising their sights, considering the vertical dimension of rooms as they plan. One design that makes ideal use of this vertical dimension is the loft bedroom opposite, but many others can be devised.

Lofts may be enclosed for privacy or left open on the sides. The open design provides better ventilation. It is also visually exciting from an architectural viewpoint. Nor are you limited to using the loft area as a bedroom. It can just as well be a secluded area for reading, TV watching, home office work, or storage. The space below the loft also seems to be separate from the rest of the room; it can be used for dining, living, or working, depending on your need.

You don't have to build a loft to make better use of the vertical space in a room. A simple project—a table that converts into a dramatic wall hanging (page 2286)—can add interest to a wall and provide extra dining space for a crowd. Another way to make use of the vertical dimension is to build a platform at one end of a long room (page 2294). This effectively turns one room into two spaces that can be treated as separate rooms. The raised space could house a home office, studio, sewing center, or whatever.

Note, however, that if you rent a house or apartment, your lease must permit you to build a platform or loft, or to mount a wall decoration. Check with your landlord before you launch any of these projects. Whether you own or rent, find out if any local building code regulations must be met in the construction of either the platform or the loft.

Make sure there are no electrical, plumbing, or other utility lines in the wall area where your fasteners will go. Such lines are usually behind the bricks in a brick wall, and between wood studs in a wood-panel, plasterboard, or plaster wall. The fasteners you use in brick do not go through the bricks, so you should have no problem with them. If you make sure the fasteners you use in other types of walls go into the studs behind the wall surface (page 2290) there will be little risk of drilling into an electrical or other utility line. Avoid drilling near any electric switch or wall outlet, or between outlets and switches that control them. If you have any doubts about the location of the wiring, confer with an electrician.

Tools and materials needed for the projects shown here include a crosscut saw; carpenter's square; bevel square; hammer; measuring tape; level; screwdriver; wood rasp; nail set; ice pick; wood chisel; safety goggles; crescent wrench for lag screws; masking tape; stapler; coarse, medium, and fine sandpaper; white glue; chalk or pencil. For fastening, you need nails in assorted sizes for assembling frame pieces and attaching them to wood wall studs, lag screws and lead expansion shields for attaching to brick walls. You will also need a ¼-inch electric drill with countersink bit and other bits to fit the size of the fasteners you will use (including carbide bits for masonry if you must drill through plaster or into brick). When buying tools keep in mind the old maxim: Good tools make work easy; poor tools just make work. Make sure the body of your electric drill has an Underwriter's Laboratory (UL) label on it—not just on the cord. Also make sure it is either double insulated or has a three-prong grounding plug, and that you use it with a grounded plug adapter if the outlet you use will not take a three-prong plug.

The lumber, fasteners, finishes, and other special materials required are listed with each of the projects that follow.

Jarrett W. Jason Strawn has a Master of Fine Arts degree and is a teacher and designer. He is also a sculptor specializing in large-scale works in a variety of media, including wood, metal, ceramics, and plastics. He works in New York, but his designs have been shown in numerous exhibits and are in public and private collections throughout the United States.

Idle space above eye level in a high-ceilinged room is used for a loft sleeping space. The supporting posts set off the space below as a dining area. Three of the four supporting posts are anchored solidly to the walls; the fourth is kept rigid with angle braces. Flooring for this 6-by-8-foot loft was cut from two 4-by-8-foot plywood panels.

When the dining table (right) is not in use, the top becomes a wall hanging, made by covering the bottom side with a colorful fabric. Molding conceals the fabric edges. Removable pegs near the top of the sides are used to make the conversion.

A generously large dining table is made from a hollow-core door that rests on two sawhorses. The sawhorses are assembled with special brackets. You can fold them for closet storage between uses.

Furniture and Finishes
Table becomes wall hanging $ ▢ ⋏ ✈

In a small house, a large dining table that is needed only for an occasional dinner party is a space-eating luxury. If you face that problem, why not hang the dining table on the wall between parties? That's the idea behind the dual-purpose space saver shown here. One side of the table is a dining surface (above); on the other side is a dramatic wall hanging made of fabric (above, left). The table top is a light, hollow-core interior door. If you rest it on two fold-up sawhorses, as shown, it can be set up any place where there is room and a need for it, even outdoors. When not in use, the sawhorses can be tucked away in a closet (photograph 1).

The sawhorses eliminate any need to make holes in the bottom of the table top for mounting legs. For the same reason—to keep both surfaces unbroken—dowel pegs that fit into holes in the edges are used to hang the table top on the wall. To take the table top down, lift the loops off the hangers, lower the table and remove the pegs (Figure A, opposite).

To make this unit, you will need a 1⅜-by-36-by-84-inch hollow-core interior door (for the table); a total of 26 feet, 1 inch of 2-by-4-inch lumber (for the sawhorses); a total of 20 feet, 1¼ inches of ¼-by-1⅜-inch wood molding; four folding metal sawhorse brackets; 9 inches of ½-inch hardwood dowel; two 1½-by-36-inch strips of sponge rubber; about 18 inches of picture wire; stapler; and primer and paint for the trim, sawhorses, and the tabletop if you paint them.

A hollow-core door this size weighs 30 pounds; the trim, cloth, pegs, and paint could add another pound. To be on the safe side, hang the table top from picture hooks designed to support 50 pounds. If the table top will be taken down frequently, hang it from screws driven in plastic anchors in plasterboard or plaster walls, or from screws driven in lead shields in brick or masonry walls.

To make the decorative hanging, cover one side of the table top with a fabric that has an interesting pattern. You will need about 2½ yards of cloth 37 inches wide.

As Figure A shows, construction is simple. From the wood molding, cut two pieces 36 inches long and two pieces 84½ inches long. Temporarily nail the shorter pieces in place so that they are flush with the sides and ends of the door edges. On each one, measure down 3 inches from what will be the top of the wall hanging. Drill centered holes at those points with a ½-inch bit, drilling about 3 inches deep. Roll a piece of sandpaper around a pencil or small dowel and use it to smooth the holes. Cut two 4⅛-inch sections of ½-inch dowel. Test the dowel sections in the holes, sanding each dowel until it fits snugly in its hole but can be readily withdrawn.

To cover one side of the door with cloth, remove the trim nailed on temporarily; then staple the cloth to the edges as in Figure A, working from the middle of each edge toward its ends and alternating sides for a smooth, tight fit. Trim away excess fabric at the corners as necessary. (The fabric could also be glued to the table top with white glue, but the cover would be harder to change later.)

After sanding, coat the wood molding and the outer ends of the dowel pegs with primer and paint. When the paint is dry, glue and nail the trim in place to cover the raw edges of fabric. Remember to line up the dowel holes, and cut away any fabric that might block them.

The Sawhorses
Assembling sawhorses with hinged brackets is easy. Two 2-by-4 legs fit into each bracket; then each pair of brackets can be spread apart at the bottom so the top grips a 2-by-4 crosspiece (photograph 2). When not in use, brackets may be spread to release the crosspiece, then be folded flat for compact storage. To support a table of standard dining height, cut eight 30-inch pieces of 2-by-4 for sawhorse legs and two 36-inch crosspieces. Fit the legs and crosspieces into the brackets, following instructions that come with the brackets. Double-headed nails, designed for easy pulling, can be used to hold the 2-by-4s in place. To protect the fabric side of the table top when it is resting on the sawhorses, glue a strip of sponge rubber atop the crosspiece of each sawhorse.

Hanging the Table Top
Decide where you want the wall hanging to be. Then, with someone's help, hold the table top against the wall with a level on its top edge. When the level reads true, lightly mark the wall about 6 inches in from either top corner. Lower the table top; then extend these lines 1/16 inch beyond each corner point. Using a square, draw short lines perpendicular to the outer end of each horizontal line. These will indicate where to mount the picture hangers. Position them so the hooks (or screwheads) will just clear the top of the hanging.

Loop picture wire around each ½-inch dowel and knot it tightly. Form another loop 3¾ inches away. One loop fits over a dowel peg, the other over a picture hook or screwhead. To put up the wall hanging, boost it into place and slide the dowel pegs through the lower wire loops into their holes.

Figure A: Cut and tack on the end moldings so you can drill holes for the dowel pegs through the moldings and into the frame of the hollow-core door. Then remove the moldings and cover one side of the door with fabric, stapling it on around the edges. Glue and nail the molding strips to the edges of the door so they conceal the fabric edges. Wires between the dowels and two heavy-duty picture hangers support the door when it is hung on the wall.

A

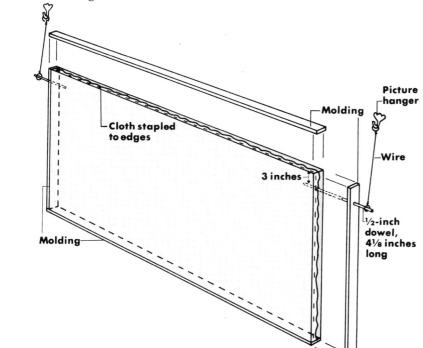

Picture hanger

Molding

Cloth stapled to edges

Wire

3 inches

½-inch dowel, 4⅛ inches long

Molding

1: When the sawhorse legs are folded for storage, they make a compact package that you can tuck in a closet, along with the crosspieces that are clamped in the brackets when in use.

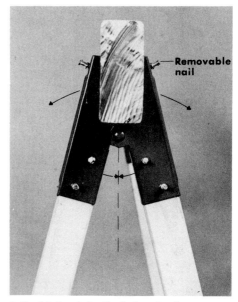

Removable nail

2: Double-headed nails, designed so they are easy to pull, fix the sawhorse legs to the crosspiece for stability. When the top nails are removed, the brackets fold as the arrows show.

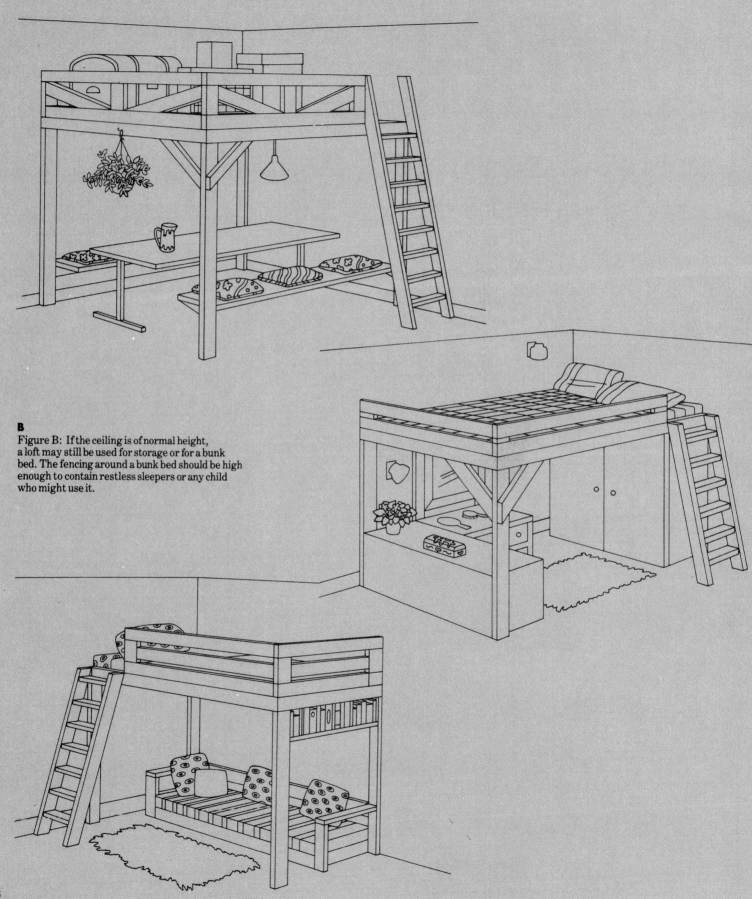

B
Figure B: If the ceiling is of normal height,
a loft may still be used for storage or for a bunk
bed. The fencing around a bunk bed should be high
enough to contain restless sleepers or any child
who might use it.

Furniture and Finishes
Building a loft

A loft of the kind pictured on page 2284 is a small raised platform built into present living space, but high enough so the space below continues to be usable. The loft may be a sleeping space, lounge, or storage area. Many old houses or apartments (particularly those in commercial buildings that have been converted) have ceilings 12 feet or more high. These are ideal for lofts, allowing almost a 6-foot height in the loft and 6-foot or better height in the area below. In some newer houses with 8-foot ceilings, a loft can serve as a storage or bunk deck, with the space beneath still usable (Figure B).

You will have to fit your loft to your needs and the space available, but the basic structure described here is adequate for a loft up to 8 feet wide or 8 feet long. The loft can easily be made longer or shorter, wider or narrower, higher or lower. It consists of a rectangular horizontal frame of 2-by-4s called joists (Figure C), supported by four vertical 2-by-4 posts. (If the loft will carry more than 600 pounds, substitute 4-by-4s for the 2-by-4 posts.) The frame is strengthened with 2-by-4 crosspieces called spacers. The loft's plywood floor is nailed to the joists and spacers. A ladder leading to the loft and a loft fence complete the project.

How you build the loft will be dictated by the walls to which two of the loft's joists will be attached. If they are plaster or plasterboard over wood studs, the job can be done quite easily with nails. But I advise you not to build a loft of this type against a wall made of plaster over metal lath and metal studs, a form of construction found in some newer residential buildings. Lofts can also be built against walls of brick or other masonry, if you use the type of fastener designed for that wall (page 2291).

Build the frame of the loft of select- or clear-grade fir, spruce or hemlock 2-by-4s (the actual size of a 2-by-4 is 1½ by 3½ inches). As shown in Figure C, order enough for the four joists, the four posts, the two angled braces, the spacers (not more than 2 feet apart), the ladder treads and side rails, and the loft fence. Use 1-by-2-inch lumber for the cleats supporting the ladder steps. The amount of 2-by-4 lumber you need will depend on the dimensions of your loft and the height of the ladder. Its steps should be 18 inches wide and about 10 inches apart (Figure K, page 2293).

Figure C: The basic framework for a loft consists of four horizontal joists with spacers between and four vertical posts. Here, two joists (*a* and *b*) are fastened to walls, as are three of the four posts. Two angled braces strengthen the freestanding post. The length and width of a loft can be adjusted to fit available space.

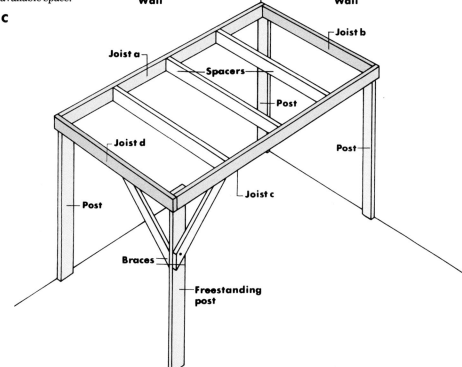

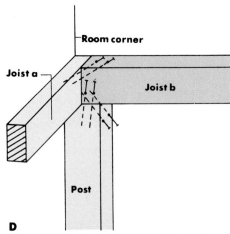

D

Figure D: Starting in the corner where the two room walls meet, joist *b* is nailed to joist *a* with nails driven at an angle (toenailed) for extra strength. After the post is in place under joist *b*, it is toenailed to joist *b* as shown.

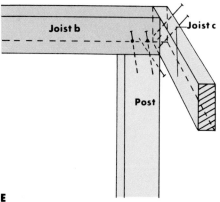

E

Figure E: Joist *c* butts against joist *b* and the two joists are toenailed to each other as above, after the post has been fitted under joist *b* and attached to the wall.

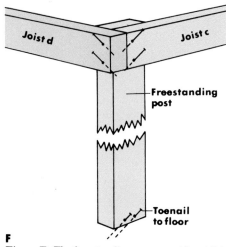

F

Figure F: The freestanding corner post is cut 3½ inches longer than the posts that attach to the walls so that joists *c* and *d* can be nailed to it. All posts are toenailed to the floor.

Make the loft floor of ¾-inch plywood. It comes in 4-by-8-foot sheets. If you make your loft this size, you will avoid cutting and fitting and still have enough room in the loft for a single or three-quarter-size bed, with some room to maneuver beside it. But if you want a larger or smaller loft, you will need to cut plywood panels to cover the frame you build.

You will need 8-, 10-, and 12- or 16-penny common nails, to assemble the frame and attach it to the stud walls. (Use 12-penny nails through thin plaster, 16-penny if it is more than ¾ inch thick.) If a vertical support doesn't happen to coincide with a stud (they rarely do), fasten it to the wall with ⅜-inch diameter toggle wing bolts, 4 inches long for walls 1 inch or less thick, 6 inches long for thicker walls. If the wall is brick or concrete block, use ⅜-inch lag screws with lead shields. Fasten ladder treads to their side rails with ¼-by-3-inch lag screws with washers. Attach cleats under the steps with white glue and 4-penny finishing nails. Nail plywood flooring to joists and spacers with 6-penny box nails.

To finish the loft, you will need sandpaper in coarse, medium, and fine grades. For a natural finish, fill imperfections with water-mix wood filler and protect the wood with acrylic stain and satin-finish polyurethane. For an opaque-colored finish, use wood plastic or spackle to fill holes, water-based latex primer and semi-gloss latex enamel to finish the wood.

Making Your Plan

Measure the room in which you will build your loft and make several sketches of possible loft arrangements. The location of doors, windows, and closets may determine where a loft can be placed. The bed—if the loft is to be a sleeping area—may determine the shape and location of the loft; allow about 3½ by 6¾ feet for a single bed, 4¾ by 6¾ feet for a full-size double bed. To this you will want to add a place to stand while you make the bed, unless you plan a bunk bed arrangement (Figure B, page 2288). In determining the heights of the loft area and the space below, subtract 4¼ inches for the structure between the spaces. You can add book shelves (page 2284), molding (Figure L, page 2293), or other decorative touches.

If your loft will differ substantially from the one shown in Figure C (page 2289), make a scale drawing of it to follow as you build. A good scale is ¾ inch on the drawing to 1 foot of actual space; that makes 1/16 inch on the drawing equal 1 inch in the loft. From the drawing, make a list of the lumber and other materials needed.

Framing the Loft

Use a straight length of 2-by-4 as a straightedge for marking the position of the longer joist that fits against the wall (joist *a* in Figure C). With a helper, hold it against the wall, ¾ inch below the height of the loft floor. Check the joist with a level; then mark along the top and bottom edges with chalk or a pencil. In the same way, position and mark the shorter joist *b* in Figure C.

Attaching Joists to Wall Studs

Vertical wood studs within a wall are usually 16 inches apart, center to center. Since you will fasten two joists to these studs, you must locate the studs exactly. If there is no visible indication of where they are, tap with a hammer handle between the pencil lines marking the joist positions. A higher pitched sound signals the solidity of a stud. Confirm the stud's location by drilling a small hole through the plaster or plasterboard. If you meet resistance after going through the outer wall, and wood dust shows on the drill tip, you have found the stud. Drill small holes ½ inch from each side of the first hole. If you find wood on both sides, your first hole is adequately centered. If not, drill additional holes until you have the center of the stud located. From this position, measure 16 inches horizontally and test-drill to locate the next stud. Repeat until you have located all the studs behind the positions of the two wall-mounted joists. Mark where the edges of each stud intersect the joist lines.

Select a long 2-by-4 and make sure one end is square. From this end, measure the length of joist *a* (Figure C); it should be 1½ inches shorter than the length of your loft floor. Use the square to mark the cutoff line and saw off the 2-by-4, keeping the saw blade to the outside of the pencil line. Rasp or sand the cut end smooth.

Hold joist *a* in position on the wall. On the joist, mark the location of each stud.

Take down the joist and drill holes for the 12- or 16-penny nails that will go into each stud using a bit slightly smaller than the nail's diameter. Make only one hole for each stud, centering it on the joist and between the marks indicating the stud's location. Place the joist back against the wall and use an ice pick or nail pushed through each hole to mark the nailing location on the wall beneath. Remove the joist, put small pieces of masking tape over the marks, which will show through the tape. Drill through the marks 1 to 1½ inches into the stud. Put joist a against the wall and drive 12- or 16-penny nails through the drilled holes into each stud.

Cut joist b (Figure C) 3 inches shorter than the width of the loft floor, since it will fit between joists a and c. Make sure both ends are square. Mount joist b on the wall as you did joist a, butting it against joist a at the corner where the two walls meet. Drive 10-penny nails at a 45-degree angle through joist b into joist a from the side and the top (Figure D). This method, known as toenailing, draws a joint together and holds tenaciously.

Mounting Joists on Masonry
If the joists must be attached to walls of brick or concrete block, there will be no studs to locate. But avoid putting fasteners into mortar joints. Mark the positions for joists a and b on the walls and saw them to length, as explained on the previous page. At 16-inch intervals, drill ⅜-inch holes along the center line of each joist to receive lag screws. Hold each joist against the wall so you can use an ice pick or nail to mark the location for the lead shields into which the lag screws will go. (Lead shields are soft lead tubes that are inserted into holes in masonry; as screws are driven into them, they expand to grip the masonry walls.) If marks coincide with mortar joints, adjust the locations just enough for the fasteners to go into solid masonry instead.

Remove the joists and put masking tape over the marks. Wearing safety goggles, drill through each hole into the masonry a distance of 2 to 2½ inches, using a masonry carbide bit matched to the size of the lead shields you will insert to receive ⅜-inch diameter, 4- or 6-inch lag screws. Choose a screw length that will go 2 to 2½ inches into the brick after passing through the joist and any interior plaster wall, if there is one over the bricks.

With all holes drilled, tap a lead shield into each one. Then place each joist in position and insert the ⅜-inch lag screws, equipped with washers. Using a crescent wrench, tighten each fastener a little at a time, moving from one to another until all are secure. Be careful not to drive them in so far that you split the joist or strip the lead shields.

Installing the Posts
With joists a and b in place, measure and cut the three 2-by-4 posts that will fit snugly under joists a and b and against the walls (Figure D, E and G). A slightly jammed fit is important. The posts must also fit tight against the walls and the floor. If there is a baseboard molding that interferes, you can remove it or saw out sections of it so the posts will fit. Or, if the baseboard is not more than ½ inch thick, notch the base of the post to bypass it (Figure H).

Fit the three posts under joists a and b, use a level to make sure they are vertical, and attach them to the walls with two fasteners, equally spaced between the joist and the floor. If the vertical posts do not coincide with a wall stud, as often happens, anchor them to the wall with toggle wing bolts, being very careful not to drill where there might be utility lines. Using 10-penny nails, toenail each joist to the post below it, and toenail the post to the floor.

To complete the support structure, cut a 2-by-4 to match the length of joist a; it will be joist c (Figure C). Cut another 3 inches longer than joist b; it will be joist d, and it is longer so it will overlap the ends of joists a and c, making the structure stronger and more attractive. Rasp or sand the ends of the 2-by-4s until they are square.

With someone helping, put one end of joist c against the outer end of joist b, butting the two pieces at a right angle (Figure E). Do not nail them together. Place a level atop joist c and adjust the joist until the level reads true. Place a 2-by-4 post against and perpendicular to joist c, and mark the upper point where joist c crosses it (Figure F). Lay both pieces on the floor and saw off the post at the mark, making

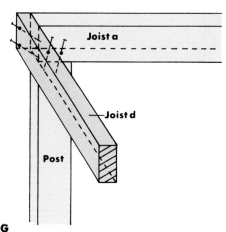

G
Figure G: With the post fixed to the wall under joist a, joist a is toenailed to it as shown. Then joist d is toenailed to joist a and the post.

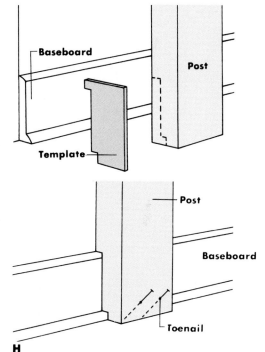

H
Figure H: If a baseboard is no more than ½ inch thick, you can notch the upright posts so they will fit flush against the wall. If the baseboard is thicker than ½ inch, remove it and cut a section from it that will let the post fit against the wall; then reinstall the sections of baseboard.

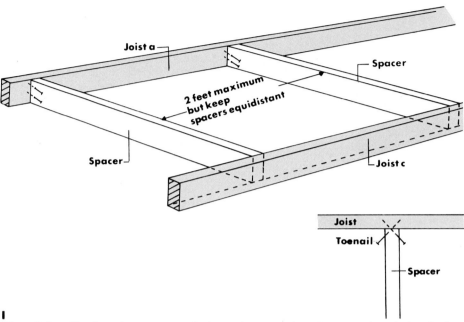

I

Figure I: Install horizontal spacers at regular intervals no more than 2 feet apart along the length of a loft. The detail at right shows how nails are driven at an angle (toenailed) through the spacer and into the wall joist *a* and freestanding joist *c*.

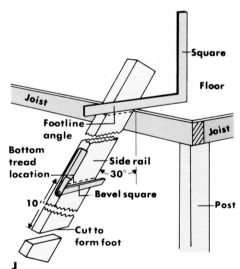

J

Figure J: With a 2-by-4 ladder side rail leaned against the loft at a safe climbing angle (no steeper than 30 degrees), lay a square on the loft floor and mark where it crosses the side rail. Set this angle on a bevel square to mark the cutoff line at the bottom of the side rail. Moving up from the bottom, draw lines at the same angle every 10 inches to locate the bottom of each tread.

sure your cut is square. Still working on the floor, place joist *c* on the upper end of the post so the two pieces form a right angle and the ends are flush; use a square to check the angle. Nail joist *c* to the post with two 10-penny nails.

Stand the assembled right angle upright so the free end of joist *c* laps the free end of joist *b*, forming a right angle. Nail joist *c* to joist *b*, using two 10-penny nails driven at a 45-degree angle through joist *c* into the end of joist *b*. With your helper continuing to support the freestanding post, place joist *d* in position and nail it to joist *a*, joist *c* and its supporting post (Figures F and G, pages 2290 and 2291). Check the structure with a square; then toenail the freestanding post to the floor with two 10-penny nails (Figure F).

For extra strength, add two diagonal braces to the freestanding corner of the loft (Figure C, page 2289). Lay lengths of 2-by-4 diagonally across the corners, using a bevel square set at a 45-degree angle as a guide. Mark where each diagonal board crosses or meets the post, and where it meets the lower edge of a joist. Cut off along these marks and nail the braces to the post and the joists with 10-penny nails.

Installing the Spacers

The horizontal spacers between joists *a* and *c* should be evenly spaced at no more than 2-foot intervals (Figure I). Cut them from 2-by-4s to fit snugly and squarely after the ends have been rasped or sanded. Temporarily nail each spacer in place, using one 10-penny nail driven directly through joist *c* into one end. Then toenail two 10-penny nails, one in from one side, the other from the opposite side, at the other end into joist *a*. Toenail the temporarily nailed spacer end at joist *c*, using one nail on each side. Keep the spacers square and flush with joists as you nail.

Installing the Loft Floor

The ¾-inch panel of fir plywood used for the floor immensely strengthens the loft as it is nailed in place. Select the side you want to have facing up; you will probably want the best side down since it will be visible from the living space below. Lay the panel atop the frame, pushing it tightly into the corner. On the bottom side, mark any overhanging surplus that needs to be trimmed off. Cover the marked lines with masking tape to minimize the tendency of plywood to splinter as you saw it. Saw off the excess wood; then sand the cut edges. Fit the plywood in place and nail it down with 6-penny box nails, placing the nails 18 inches apart along all joists and spacers.

If one sheet of plywood does not cover the loft floor area, cut what you need from a second sheet to fill in the extra space. But use as few seams as possible, and make sure they meet on a joist or spacer so all edges can be nailed down.

Fencing the Loft

Putting a fence around a loft makes it safer to use and often more attractive to look at. Make the fence of 2-by-4s for maximum strength. Cut four 2-by-4s to the length and width of the loft. Nail two of them to each other and to the floor and loft joist around the edge of the loft (Figure B, center, page 2288). Cut upright posts and toenail them to the boards nailed to the floor. Toenail the second pair of horizontal fence pieces to the upright posts. Toenail any fence parts that touch a wall to the wall. If diagonal pieces go between the horizontal pieces (as in Figure B, top, page 2288) place 2-by-4s against the post and the floor board the diagonal will join to. Mark the lines of intersection, and saw the diagonal piece to these lines. Fit diagonal in place and toenail it to posts and floorboard.

The Loft Ladder

Save the best 2-by-4s you have for the loft ladder. Lean one 2-by-4 that you will use as a side rail against the loft at the angle you want the ladder to be, but no steeper than 30 degrees for safety and comfort. Place a square or straightedge on the loft floor, extending over the 2-by-4, and draw a horizontal line, as in Figure J. Set an adjustable bevel square at this angle; it will be the angle at which you will cut the bottom of the ladder rails and the angle at which the treads will meet the side rails. Mark the angle cut near the bottom of the 2-by-4 and saw it off; then lean the 2-by-4 against the loft again to test the accuracy of the cut. Cut the base on the second side rail, using the first as a pattern.

With the bevel square still at the same angle, measure up from the base of the side rails and draw lines every 10 inches to mark the position for the underside of each stair tread, also the top of each supporting cleat (Figure K). Extend the lines around the rails to locate where lag screws will go through into the treads.

How far the side rails extend above the loft floor is a personal choice; on the loft shown on page 2284, I let them extend several feet to provide a comfortable hand-hold for the climber entering or leaving the loft.

Cut cleats to support the treads from 1-by-2-inch fir or pine, long enough to fit along the line marked on the side rail without projecting at either edge. Use white glue and 4-penny finishing nails, two to each cleat, to fasten the cleats to the side rails (Figure K). Let the glue dry thoroughly. Cut the treads from 2-by-4s, making sure the ends are square. Treads that measure 18 inches from end to end are comfortable, but you can make them 14 or even 12 inches if space is limited.

Drill 3/16-inch holes through each side rail, centering them ¾ inch above the lines marking the top of the cleats. As you drill, hold scrap wood just above the cleat to minimize wood splintering as the drill comes through. When both rails have been drilled for all the treads that will attach to them, place treads on top of the cleats and temporarily nail the treads in place with 8-penny finishing nails. Then lay the ladder on the floor, bracing it against a wall, and drill through the holes in the side rails into the ends of the treads. Use a 3/16-inch bit and drill about 1 inch into each tread. Install ¼-by-3-inch lag screws in these holes with washers under the heads. Tighten the lag screws with a crescent wrench.

Place the ladder in position against the loft, and toenail the ladder to both the loft and the floor with 10-penny finishing nails. For extra safety, you can toenail two 8-penny finishing nails through each tread end into the side rail.

Finishing the Loft

Molding added to the edges of the loft (Figure L) will hide the plywood edges and joints, improving the appearance. Sand all rough spots with coarse, then medium, then fine-grade sandpaper. If you plan to stain the loft for a natural-wood look, fill holes and blemishes with a water-mix wood filler. Then smooth with fine-grade sandpaper, clean off the dust, and apply an acrylic stain. Let this dry, sand lightly, dust, and apply two coats of satin-finish polyurethane.

If you plan to paint, smooth with fine-grade sandpaper, and fill all holes or blemishes with wood plastic or spackle. Then sand, dust, and apply a coat of water-based latex primer, followed by two coats of semigloss latex enamel.

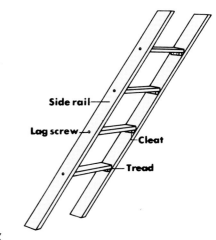

K

Figure K: Line up the tops of the ladder cleats with the lines marking the bottom of the treads, and fasten the cleats to the side rails with glue and nails. Then rest the treads on top of cleats and fasten them to the side rails with lag screws.

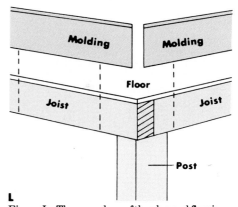

L

Figure L: The raw edges of the plywood flooring and the 2-by-4 joints can be concealed with plain or decorative molding, glued and nailed to the loft joists as shown.

A platform built into one end of a long, narrow room visually creates a separate area that can be used as a home office, studio, library, or sewing center. Here, the carpeting conceals the carpentry below so it needs only be sturdy, not of cabinetmaker quality.

Two platform levels, as shown in this platform that is being built, can make an even more dramatic difference in a room's appearance than a one-level platform. Each step here is 4½ inches high.

Furniture and Finishes
Platforms for rooms

$ ● ♦ ✈

As many-tiered oriental houses and modern split-levels attest, a variety of levels within a structure dramatically changes the feeling of living space. A raised platform built within a room is the simplest and most economical way to make the most of the vertical dimension. All you do is build a new floor on top of the present one (opposite, above). The height of a new level may vary, but for safety's sake it should be high enough so no one can miss seeing it, yet low enough so the step up is comfortable. I suggest a rise of 4 to 6 inches in a room of average size. If you want a more dramatic change, you might try two or even three levels, each a comfortable distance apart (opposite, below). You don't want to feel like you are walking a tightrope or teetering on the edge.

Design and Construction

First decide what part of an existing room you want raised to the new level. One-third to two-fifths of the floor area is a good rule of thumb. Then decide whether you want more than one new level, and if so, how high each rise should be. Consider, too, that a platform does not have to involve three walls; it can adjoin two in a corner, or even project from one like a peninsula. Check the materials in the walls, floor, and baseboard; the location of electric lines and outlets; the position of radiators, registers, or other elements of the room that affect the platform design. Keep these in mind as you make your plan.

The platform, like the floor on which it is built, must have adequate support. That support comes from a framework of 2-by-4s, consisting of sole boards nailed flat against the floor, vertical posts nailed to the sole boards, and horizontal joists nailed to the posts (Figure M). The joists are then braced with 2-by-4 spacers. Panels of ¾-inch plywood are nailed to the joists and spacers to make the raised floor. (If the floor will be covered with carpeting, linoleum, or tile, you can use 1-inch chipboard, also called particle board or pressed board, for flooring; it is cheaper than plywood, but more vulnerable to damage from impacts, heavy weights, and moisture.) The 2-by-4s used should be of select- or clear-grade fir, spruce, or hemlock.

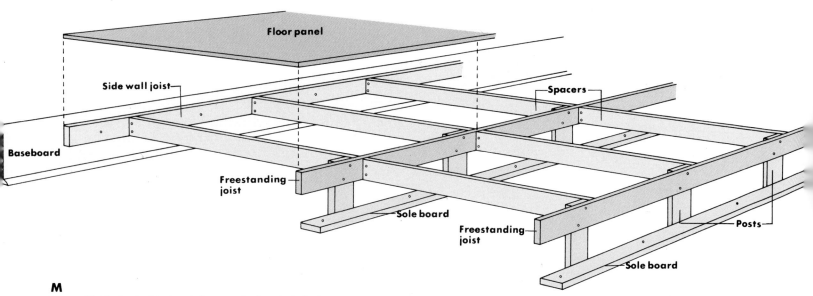

M

Figure M: The basic structure below any platform includes horizontal joists running across the length of the platform, supported by vertical posts nailed to sole boards that are nailed to the existing floor. Spacers between the joists across the narrower width dimension strengthen the framework and provide additional surfaces to which floor panels can be nailed.

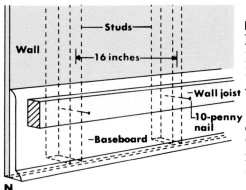

N

Figure N; Wall joists may be nailed to baseboards if the baseboard is flat and high enough for the joist to fit flat snugly against it. Nails should go through the baseboard into studs in the existing wall (page 2290); often nail heads visible in the baseboard serve to locate the studs.

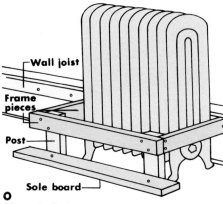

O

Figure O: To frame a radiator, bring the frame pieces out from the wall joist, leaving space to reach the radiator controls and keeping all wood 6 inches from the radiator for fire safety. Join the two projecting pieces with a horizontal crosspiece, and support this frame with posts nailed to a sole board that is nailed to the floor.

Installing Against-the-Wall Joists

Establish the position of the joists that will be nailed to the walls against which the platform will fit (Figures M, page 2295, and N). If you use three walls, as is usual, you will have a rear-wall joist running the width of the platform and two side-wall joists that extend out from the rear-wall joist to within 2½ inches of the planned front of the platform. A header joist is nailed to the fronts of the side-wall joists.

If you plan a platform height of 6 inches and a ¾-inch plywood floor, the top of each wall joist should be 5¼ inches above the old floor. If 1-inch chipboard is used, this height would be 5 inches. A low or irregular baseboard should be removed, but if the baseboard is flat and more than 6 inches high, the wall joist can be nailed to it (Figure N).

Use a straight length of 2-by-4, with a level resting on it and reading true, as a guide when you outline the positions of the wall joists with pencil or chalk. Where heat radiators or registers are located, build frames as shown in Figures O and P. Build frames around electrical outlets as in Figure Q or have an electrician raise outlets above the planned platform for easy access.

With such locations framed, fasten the wall joists to the baseboard or wall. If the wall is plaster or plasterboard over wood studs, locate the studs (page 2290) and drive one 12-penny nail through the joist into each. If the wall is of brick or concrete block, use 6-inch masonry nails spaced 12 inches apart, and wear safety goggles as you drive them. Avoid nailing near any electric outlets.

Completing the Framing

Joists that are not fastened to a wall run the longer dimension of the platform, usually front to back and parallel to the side walls. Panels of 4-by-8-foot plywood butt snugly against each other on top of these joists (Figure R). Since each panel overlaps a joist by only ¾ inch, take all measurements carefully so the panels fit together snugly. Check the actual dimensions of the 2-by-4s you use; they usually measure 1½ by 3½ inches, but if they don't, adjust accordingly.

Each freestanding joist unit (those not against a wall) includes a sole board, vertical posts and the joist (Figure S). Cut a 2-by-4 sole board to match the length of a side-wall joist. Lay it on its flat side parallel to one side wall and 47¼ inches from that wall. Holding it in this position, nail it to the floor with 12-penny common nails (if the floor is wood) or 4-inch masonry nails (if the floor is concrete), spacing the nails 18 inches apart. Next, cut and attach the vertical posts. To determine their height, measure 24¾ inches from the rear-wall baseboard along the top of each side-wall joist and make a mark. Tack a cord to one mark, stretch it tautly to the other, and tack it there (Figure T). Hold a 2-by-4 upright against the sole board just ahead of the cord, and mark where the cord crosses it. Cut the 2-by-4 at this line to make your first post. Nail this post against the sole board ahead of the cord, using two 10-penny common nails (Figure U).

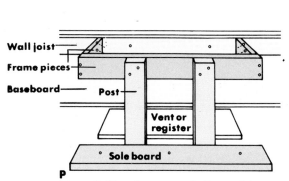

P

Figure P: If you frame around a floor register, allow room for easy access to the controls and for cleaning. When the platform flooring is laid, cut out a rectangle to make sure heat will circulate freely in the flooring.

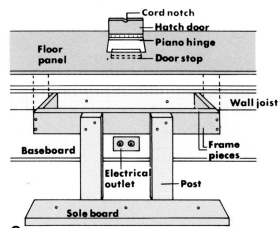

Q

Figure Q: When you frame around electrical outlets, cut only a small hole in the flooring just large enough for access to the outlet. A better but more expensive alternative: have an electrician raise the outlets above platform level.

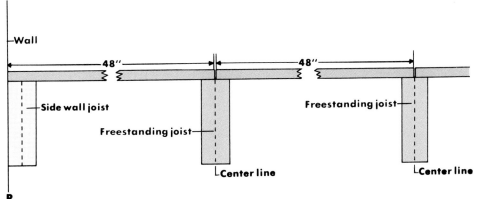

Figure R: Make sure the first flooring panel will fit in place with its outer edge centered on the free-standing joist closest to the wall. The first freestanding joist should be positioned so the edge nearest the side wall is 47¼ inches from the wall (or to the center of the joist, 48 inches).

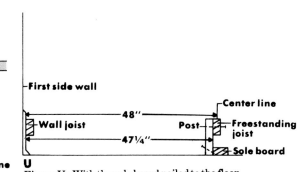

Figure U: With the sole board nailed to the floor and the vertical posts cut to length, toenail each post to the sole board, starting 24¾ inches from the rear baseboard and working toward the front of the platform. Then nail a joist to all of the vertical posts at 24-inch intervals.

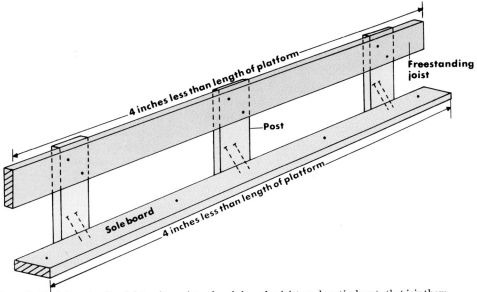

Figure S: Each freestanding joist unit consists of a sole board, a joist, and vertical posts that join them. All are cut from 2-by-4s. Cut the sole board to length, locate one edge 47¼ inches from a side wall, and nail it to the floor.

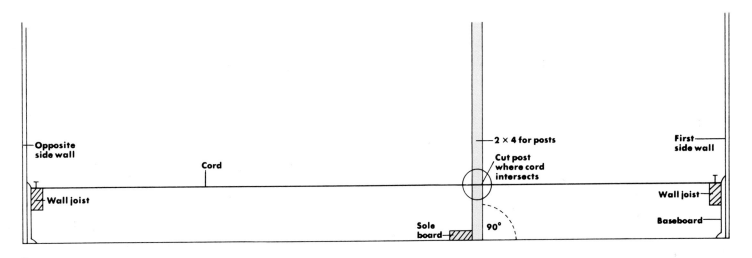

Figure T: To determine the heights of vertical posts, mark side-wall joists 24¾ inches from the rear wall baseboard. Stretch a cord tautly between the marks and tack both ends. Mark where the cord crosses a 2-by-4 held upright against the sole board. Cut off the 2-by-4 along this mark. This method, applied to all vertical posts, compensates for any unevenness in the floor.

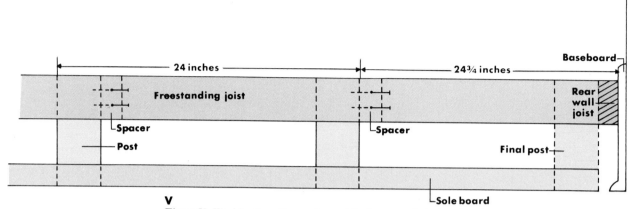

V

Figure V: Working from the rear toward the front, mark the location of a vertical post 24¾ inches from the rear wall baseboard. The remaining posts are spaced at 24-inch intervals. The crosswise spacers and final post (indicated by dotted lines) are installed after the joist units are assembled and nailed down.

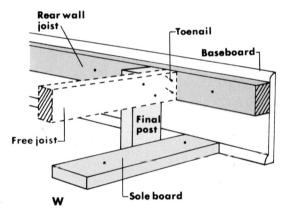

W

Figure W: Cut and install a final post to serve as a brace where it meets the rear-wall joist. Then nail the end of the freestanding joist to the top of the post and to the rear-wall joist.

Move the cord 24 inches toward the front of the platform and tack in this new position, making sure it is kept taut. Mark and cut the second post as you did the first. Continue moving the cord, cutting, and installing posts every 24 inches (Figure V) until the front of the platform is reached. (The distance between the front post and the platform front can be less but should not be more than 24 inches.) Using the top of the rear-wall joist as a guide, cut a final post to fit against that joist (Figure W).

With the posts nailed to the sole board, cut a joist to attach to the posts—the same length as the side-wall joists. With a helper, hold the joist against the vertical posts and mark where each post intersects it. Place the joist on the floor and drive two 10-penny common nails almost through it. Again with help, hold the joist so its top edge is flush with the top of the posts, brace the post with your foot, and finish driving the nails into each post. Toenail the joist to the rear-wall joist, using two 10-penny nails (Figure W).

This completes the installation of the first joist unit. Install additional joists, with their centers 48 inches apart, until the opposite side wall is reached. Depending on the width of the room, the last joist unit may be closer than 48 inches to the side wall; you will have to trim a 48-inch wide panel of flooring to fit the space. If you plan to place a heavy object such as a piano on the platform area, install an extra joist unit midway between those in place to provide an extra support under the area where the extra weight will be.

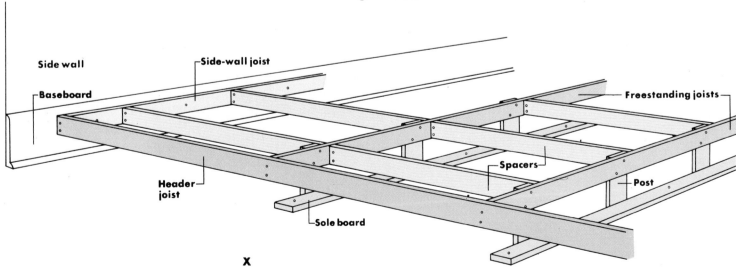

X

Figure X: When all joists are in place, cut and nail spacers and then a header joist to fit across the front of the frame. Nail the header joist to each side-wall joist and all intervening joists.

When all joists are in place, cut and install spacers to fit snugly between the joists (Figure X). Starting at the rear wall, fit the first spacer between the side-wall joist and the nearest free joist, butting it snugly against the post that is 24¾ inches from the rear wall. Drive two equally spaced 10-penny nails through the joist into one end of the spacer, while holding the spacer flush with the top of the joist. Toenail the other end of the spacer to the side-wall joist using two 10-penny nails. Then toenail the opposite side of the spacer into the side-wall joist using two nails. Moving toward the front of the platform, install a spacer against the next vertical post and between the side-wall joist and the free joist. Repeat between other joists.

With the final spacer in place, install the header joist that runs across the front of the platform (Figure X). Nail it to the ends of both side-wall joists and all the intervening joists, using two 10-penny nails at each point. From scrap wood, cut small blocks the thickness of the header joist, butt them against the front of each sole board, and nail them to the floor (Figure Y). This completes the framing.

Before installing the flooring, mark the walls to indicate the position of joists and spacers. When the flooring is down, you can use these marks to draw guidelines for nailing down the flooring.

Place the first 4-by-8-foot plywood panel at a rear corner of the platform, making sure the long edge matches the center line of the freestanding joist. If it doesn't, the wall corner is not square and you will have to trim the panel to fit it. Work cautiously and remove plywood a little at a time from the sides that fit against the walls until a proper alignment on the center line of the joist and the spacer is reached. The next flooring panel will then drop into place with one edge butted against the first panel and the other edge lined up with the center line of the next freestanding joist. Cut the final panel to fill the space between the last freestanding joist and the opposite side wall. With the flooring in place, draw lines from the marks on the walls across the flooring to indicate the positions of each joist and spacer. These will show you where to nail through the flooring.

Until all panels have been fitted into place, nail each panel down with two 8-penny box nails on each joist. When you are satisfied with the fit, nail with 8-penny box nails every 12 inches to both joists and spacers.

The flooring should overhang the header joist by 1 inch for ¾-inch plywood, or 1¼ inches for chipboard panels. Cut a board of either floor panel material to fit under this overhang, standing on edge (Figure Y). Nail this strip to the header joist and to the scrap blocks at the bottom using 8-penny common box nails spaced 12 inches apart.

To cover all raw edges, if you want them hidden, add molding strips (Figure Z). But if you plan to cover the platform with carpeting, linoleum, or tile, install the floor covering; then use trims or moldings designed to go with the covering used.

For related projects, see "Models and Mockups," "Plywood and Foam Furnishings," and "Supergraphics."

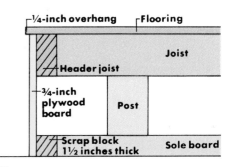

Y

Figure Y: After flooring panels are laid, cut a strip of floor paneling and nail it to the header joist and to the scrap blocks that have been nailed to the floor in front of the sole boards.

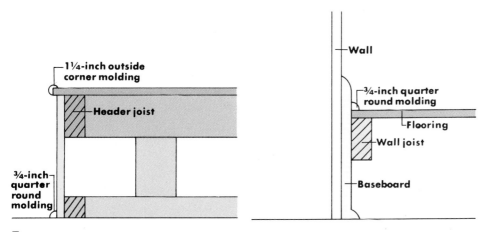

Z

Figure Z: For a finished appearance, add molding to the front edge of the platform flooring and along the base of the platform (left), as well as along the rear and sides (right). If you use a floor covering, use the trim designed for it.

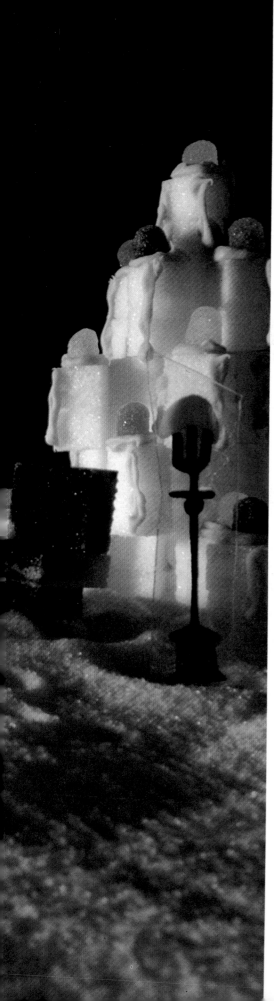

SUGAR SHAPES
What a Sweet Idea

Armando Risbano, consultant for this entry, teaches at the Food and Maritime Trade High School in New York. He is in charge of the student-operated cafeteria (the students also cater for city agencies) and evening classes for people in the food trade. He was an assistant chef at New York's Waldorf-Astoria Hotel and mess sergeant at the Cooks and Bakers School for the U. S. Army. He is a member of the International Chef's Association, Inc.

You don't need a sweet tooth to appreciate centerpieces and party favors made of sugar. They are primarily designed to appeal to the eyes rather than the tastebuds. Still, if you or your child has an uncontrollable urge to nibble, sugar shapes such as those pictured at left (though not the acetate cutout figures) are pure candy and completely edible.

Start With Sugar

Sugar comes in several forms that can be used to make fanciful decorations:

Granulated sugar, white or brown, can be sprinkled to simulate snow or sand. Both can also be mixed with egg white (one egg white to every pound of sugar) to make a malleable paste for molding figures. No cooking is necessary. Simply set the mold aside until the paste hardens; then unmold the shape and decorate it.

Sugar cubes and sugar tablets make ideal building blocks for houses, wedding chapels, castles, trees, park benches, fences, or animals. The cubes are square and the tablets are shaped like dominoes; otherwise they are the same.

Powdered or confectioner's sugar, which comes packed with a small amount of cornstarch to prevent caking, can be mixed with egg white (one egg white to every pound of sugar) to make an uncooked icing. Use an electric mixer at high speed, and add a few drops of water if it is needed to soften the icing. This icing can be used as mortar to hold the sugar bricks together, or it can be squeezed through a pastry tube to decorate the molded shapes.

Granulated sugar substitutes that pour and can be measured the same way as sugar may be used in place of sugar when there is a need to restrict calorie intake. The substitutes are more expensive, however, and do not taste quite the same.

Mold It and Decorate It

Use shallow, simple molds for making sugar-paste figures. Try individual gelatin molds, small cookie cutters, metal or plastic toys, or small ornaments. Make molds for special shapes or larger figures using strips of waxed cardboard cut from milk cartons (page 2304). To build a sugar-cube house, use a framework of cardboard or a block of plastic foam to provide support for the structure.

Brown or white sugar pastes can be used to mold many things. If you want more color, food coloring is an ideal paint. These dyes are perfectly safe to eat. Use the primary colors as they come in the bottles, or mix them to achieve other colors. To color icing or a granulated-sugar paste, add a few drops of food color as you mix. You can also brush color on a finished figure or sugar-cube structure, using a small watercolor brush dipped into food coloring.

If the guests include nibblers, you may want to flavor the granulated-sugar paste with a few drops of pure liquid extract, available in a variety of flavors including vanilla, peppermint, and lemon.

To decorate your assemblages, add gumdrops, licorice strings, lollipops, cookies, other candies; if you use such nonedibles as tiny dolls, flowers (real or artificial), yarn, ribbon, or cutouts from magazines, make sure no one will be tempted to eat them by mistake.

This skaters' wonderland, with sugar-cube trees and snowdrifts of granulated sugar, could be a centerpiece for a winter party. Or, if you make it for a summer buffet, it will make your guests feel ten degrees cooler. Directions start on page 2302.

This sugar-tablet schoolhouse could mark the opening or closing of school; with a few modifications it could become a wedding chapel for a bridal shower or a house for a housewarming.

Kitchen Favorites and Celebrations
A sugar wonderland

The next time you have friends in for cocoa on a frosty morning, surprise them with a charming scene of old-fashioned skaters on a pond (page 2300).

Spread a layer of newspapers on your work surface to catch excess sugar. Cover these newspapers with waxed paper to keep the frosted sugar shapes from sticking. Assemble this sugar wonderland, or any such large scene, inside a shallow box lid to make it easier to move.

Here you can improvise to your heart's content. In the scene pictured, the pond is an unframed mirror. The skaters, snowman, and street lamp are acetate cutouts available at toy stores. You could substitute tiny dolls and miniature plastic toys. To duplicate this scene, put a mirror in the middle of the box lid. Surround it with mounds of sugar to simulate a snow-covered landscape. Use your fingertips to make tiny footprints leading to the edge of the mirror. For a park bench, use two sugar tablets for the seat and one cube for the base, cementing them together with drops of powdered-sugar icing. Paint the bench green with food coloring, but leave its edges snow-white.

Build the trees with sugar cubes and tablets in whatever arrangements you like, using a small amount of powdered-sugar icing to hold them together. Some trees can be made by simply stacking the cubes in ever-decreasing numbers from the base up. As you near the top, cut sugar tablets into smaller pieces, using a hacksaw or a serrated knife sawing across the tablet. (Using a straight-edged knife or kitchen shears will splinter and crack the tablet.) Decorate the trees with garlands of green-tinted icing and gumdrops, as shown, or paint them with food coloring.

When the scene is complete, move it to the table where it is to be displayed. If minor touching up is needed, conceal the edges of the box lid with more sugar.

Kitchen Favorites and Celebrations
Sugar-brick schoolhouse

The miniature schoolhouse shown above, left, would be an appropriate decoration for a back-to-school or graduation party. Thick icing takes several hours to dry completely; so make this centerpiece well in advance, perhaps the night before.

The schoolhouse is built on a base of fiberboard or corrugated cardboard around a plastic-foam core. Such foam can be cut to size with a craft knife. Then slather the base with powdered-sugar icing and center the foam block on the icing. Decide where you want windows and the door; then cut them out of colored acetate, construction paper, or tissue paper, or use magazine cutouts. Cut the windows and door larger than you want them to be so edges can be covered with sugar tablets. Glue these pieces to the foam block, using white glue or icing as the adhesive around the edges.

There are three ways you can attach the sugar tablets with icing to the foam core, depending on how much time you have and the appearance you seek.

The method used to build the schoolhouse pictured is quick. Cover one side of the foam block with icing, and simply stack the tablets against the side, pressing them into the soft icing. Put a narrow border of icing around the base of the block, too, to secure the first row of sugar tablets to the base. This must be done quickly, before the icing starts to harden, or the sugar tablets will not stick. The tablets (or cubes) can be stacked in vertical piles, or they can be staggered in alternating rows like bricks. If you need to cut any tablets to fit, do so with a serrated knife or a hacksaw blade. After you have built the walls, roof, and bell tower in this manner, fill a pastry tube with pink-tinted icing and squeeze out icing to outline the sugar tablets. Or, if you prefer, tint the sugar tablets a traditional schoolhouse red with food coloring applied with a small watercolor brush.

A second way to build the schoolhouse, without having to apply icing to the foam core, is to put icing on top of each row of sugar tablets as you build. For this, fill a pastry tube with white or tinted icing, and put a thick rope of icing at the bottom edge of the foam core. Press the first row of tablets in place and repeat the process. With this technique, it is not necessary to put icing on the foam core. By applying more icing than is needed to hold the tablets together, you can make it ooze out of the cracks.

The third way is to build up the sugar tablets just the way a brick mason works with real bricks. Use the icing as mortar to fasten in place the bottom edge and one side edge of each tablet, one at a time, laying tablets in staggered rows. You do not need to put icing on the foam block.

When you have finished the basic structure, put a gumdrop bell in the tower and a teacher in the doorway. Sprinkle granulated brown sugar to make a path around the schoolhouse, squeeze a border of green-icing shrubbery in place, and add two lollipop trees. Surround the schoolhouse with mounds of granulated sugar snow.

Kitchen Favorites and Celebrations
Sweet wedding bells
¢ ⌧ 👪 🍳

Wedding bells made of sugar paste, pictured below, are pretty, easy to make, and inexpensive as party favors for a bridal shower.

With a spoon, thoroughly mix one pound of white granulated sugar with one egg white. Add a few drops of red food coloring until the paste is a medium shade of pink and add flavoring if desired. Press the paste inside metal bells such as those used for Christmas decorations (remove the clappers first). Set the filled bells aside for several hours until the exposed surface is dry to the touch. The inside will still be moist, but it is best to unmold the bell shapes before they are completely dry. To do this, tap the outside of the mold all around to loosen the outer layer of sugar; then knock the sugar bell out into your hand. If the number of molds you have is limited, cover any unused sugar paste and store it in the refrigerator until the first batch of bells is unmolded.

To make hangers for the bells, twist paper clips into S shapes, and push the bottom halves into the bell tops while they are still moist enough so they do not crack. Then let the bells stand for several hours more until they are completely dry. Tie white satin ribbons and sprays of lily of the valley to the top halves of the clips.

This ladybug family was molded in measuring spoons of graduated sizes, then was colored with food coloring (equal parts of red and green coloring make black).

Kitchen Favorites and Celebrations
Lucky ladybugs
¢ ⌧ 👪 🍳

Use leftover white sugar paste from another project to make the ladybugs shown above, right. Press the paste into four graduated measuring spoons. When the oval shapes are dry, knock them out into your hand. Tint them to look like ladybugs, using food coloring applied with a small watercolor brush. To make black, mix equal parts of red and green.

Pastel sugar bells are inexpensive, easy-to-make favors for a wedding or a New Year's Eve party.

Sugar shapes can be naturally brown as well as naturally white or tinted. The molds for these brown-sugar shapes were made with strips cut from a milk carton.

Kitchen Favorites and Celebrations
Brown-sugar shapes

Light-brown granulated sugar makes shapes that look something like gingerbread but taste much sweeter. Simple molded figures like the ones shown at left can also be made with white sugar left white or tinted with food coloring.

Make molds for sugar shapes by cutting narrow waxed cardboard strips from a milk carton. Bend, fold, and tape the strips into the shapes you want. The figure shows how to make a five-pointed star. Keep the molds small and shallow so the sugar paste will dry in several hours.

With a spoon, mix one pound of brown granulated sugar with one egg white. Place the molds on a sheet of waxed paper and press the paste inside, smoothing the top surfaces with a table knife. Let the paste dry completely; then carefully remove the molds. Decorate the shapes with white or tinted powdered-sugar icing.

Kitchen Favorites and Celebrations
Sugar place card

You can turn any molded sugar shape into a place card by writing the guest's name on it with powdered-sugar icing, squeezed through a pastry tube. The brown-sugar duck, shown below, was made in a milk-carton mold (above). Dark-brown sugar was used, and the icing was tinted pale pink. This duck can stand up, but thinner shapes can lay flat on the plate or napkin.

For related crafts and entries, see "Birthday Celebrations," "Confections and Comfits," "Christmas Celebrations," and "Gingerbread."

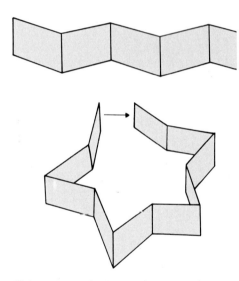

Cut a narrow strip of waxed cardboard from a milk carton; then accordion-fold the strip into ten equal parts. Bring the two ends together and attach them with cellophane tape to make a five-pointed star.

A brown-sugar duck, cast in a mold made of milk-carton strips, is decorated with sugar icing to become a place card for a children's party. Few will survive to go home as souvenirs.